Marine Chemistry

CR BRIGHTWELL

Marine Chemistry

Project Team
Editors: Ryan Greene, David E. Boruchowitz, Craig Sernotti
Copy Editor: Jessica White
Cover Design: Mary Ann Kahn

T.F.H. Publications
President/CEO: Glen S. Axelrod
Executive Vice President: Mark E. Johnson
Publisher: Christopher T. Reggio
Production Manager: Kathy Bontz

T.F.H. Publications, Inc.
One TFH Plaza
Third and Union Avenues
Neptune City, NJ 07753

Printed and Bound in China

07 08 09 10 11 1 3 5 7 9 8 6 4 2

Library of Congress Cataloging-in-Publication Data
Brightwell, Chris.
Marine chemistry : a complete guide to water chemistry for the marine aquarium / Chris Brightwell.
p. cm.
Includes bibliographical references.
ISBN-13: 978-0-7938-0574-7 (alk. paper)
1. Aquarium water. 2. Aquariums. I. Title.

SF457.5.B75 2006
639.34'2--dc22

2006026738

The Leader In Responsible Animal Care For Over 50 Years!™
www.tfhpublications.com

To my wife, Denise, for always supporting my pursuit of this hobby and profession, and whose sense of humor keeps me young at heart.

Talent is cheaper than table salt. What separates the talented individual from the successful one is a lot of hard work.

—Stephen King

The opinion of one man is only as good as his experience.

—Joseph Bates

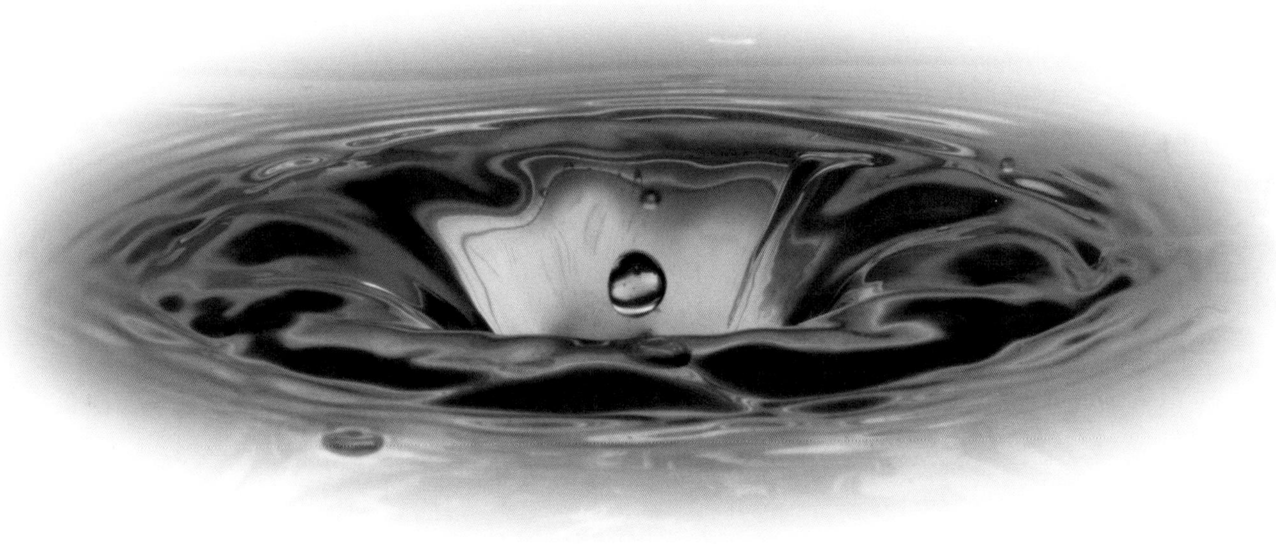

Table of Contents

Introduction

I must have sat down to work on this book over a dozen times during the past several years, but one way or another something always seemed to divert my attention away from finishing it; thankfully, deadlines established by my publisher have put an end to that cycle. I initially began writing this book because I felt that there was no truly definitive work on marine chemistry as it pertained to marine aquarium husbandry, and that such a book could help hobbyists make better decisions about the management of water quality in their aquaria. This belief was largely inspired by the countless hours that I have spent communicating with hobbyists in my professional capacity regarding questions they have with water chemistry in marine aquaria. Answering these questions often helps aquarists avoid mistakes, meaning less wasted time, money, and effort, and can increase the hobbyist's understanding of water chemistry enough to help them become more successful.

As many experienced marine aquarium hobbyists will attest, there are both similarities and differences in water chemistry between freshwater and marine environments. To generalize that the same processes are at work in both environments is often erroneous and furthermore potentially disastrous. Chemistry does not have to be difficult to understand, however, and time spent reading the works of a credible author and conversing with hobbyists of confirmed experience advance a newcomer's chances of success dramatically. I hope that this book will increase the understanding of chemistry as it applies to the marine aquarium so that all readers will benefit. The order of topics and the subject matter itself are intended to be logical and easy to follow. My goal is to make the hobby more enjoyable and successful for all marine aquarists, but particularly the novice, who is often at a loss when looking for reliable advice.

You could say my entire life has helped prepare me to write *Marine Chemistry*. The vast majority of my childhood was spent outdoors, studying wildlife, especially fish. I kept multiple aquariums and terrariums at any given time. As I grew up, my love of the outdoors enabled me to excel in the study of the various natural sciences, and I eventually undertook the task of earning a degree in marine science (encompassing the study of marine biology, marine chemistry, marine geology, and physical oceanography). During college, I specialized in chemistry, biology, ichthyology, and behavior and ecology of fishes. After graduation I was hired by a major manufacturer of aquarium chemical and filtration products and spent many years working on the research and

development of new products, providing advanced technical support to aquarium hobbyists of all skill levels, writing product informational literature, training company and retail sales personnel, and so on.

I want to make it clear that this book does not promote products manufactured by one company or another; readers will not find a single reference to a name brand or manufacturer within these pages. Instead, the information presented will better enable hobbyists to make their own informed decisions about which brands to trust or avoid. I believe that the money invested in the purchase of this book is nothing compared to what readers will save by making the right decisions about which products to trust and which to leave on the store shelves.

I would like to extend my thanks to all of the hobbyists and professionals with whom I have had contact throughout the years, whose questions I have been called upon to answer, or whose ideas and theories I have been called upon for comment. It is largely because of these exchanges that I realized the importance of a marine chemistry reference for hobbyists and began writing this book. Keep the questions coming; I will do my best to answer them!

Part One

Marine Aquarium Water Paramaters

CHAPTER 1

Water Quality

It should go without mention that the single most important contributor to success with a marine aquarium is maintaining water parameters within tolerable ranges. If the conditions are not acceptable to the livestock, they will begin to get sick and may eventually die if something is not done quickly to correct the situation. One of the reasons that it is so important to keep within bounds of water parameters is that marine organisms have evolved over the past several million years in relatively stable water conditions, so their aquarium water needs to mirror those conditions as closely as possible.

In a sense, one can think of a marine aquarium as a super-concentrated, and simplified, piece of the ocean. Seawater is quite complex in chemical make-up. It can generally be described as a soup containing water; major, minor, and trace constituents or elements; gases; nutrients; and dissolved and particulate organic compounds and materials. Artificial seawater used in marine aquaria is similar to ocean water in some respects, but different in others. By design, marine aquarium water may have higher or lower concentrations of various substances, dictated by the perceived needs of the captive stock (and often, unfortunately, by the cost of synthetic salt manufacture).

Table 1.1. Recommended Marine Aquarium Water Parameters[1]	
Temperature	72 to 78°F (22 to 25°C)
Specific Gravity (density)	1.021 to 1.026 g/cm^3
pH	8.1 to 8.4
Alkalinity	7.0 to 10.0 dKH (2.5 to 3.6 meq/L)
Carbon Dioxide (dissolved)	2.0 to 5.0 mg/L
Oxygen (dissolved)	5.0 to 8.0 mg/L
Calcium [Ca^{2+}]*	412.0 to 450.0 mg/L
Magnesium [Mg^{2+}]*	1288.0 to 1320.0 mg/L
Strontium [Sr^{2+}]*	8.0 to 10.0 mg/L
Iron [$Fe^{2+/3+}$]*	0.1 to 0.3 mg/L
Iodine [all species of I]	0.05 to 0.08 mg/L
Phosphate [all species of P]	<0.05 mg/L (immeasurable)
Silicate [all species of Si]	<0.05 mg/L (immeasurable)
Ammonia [NH_3]	0.0 mg/L (immeasurable)
Nitrite [NO^{2-}]	0.0 mg/L (immeasurable)
Nitrate [NO^{3-}]*	<10.0 mg/L

The location that a species typically inhabits in the wild (i.e. lagoon, reef flat, reef crest, reef front) will influence a few parameters to a very small extent, but in essence tropical reef inhabitants can all survive quite happily and remain healthy in a reasonable simulation of seawater. This is indeed fortunate for aquarium hobbyists because at present there are few synthetic blends of sea salt that approach natural seawater

1 Parameters marked with an asterisk indicate that they are less important to maintain within the recommended ranges in fish-only systems. All other parameters should be adhered to as closely as possible, and all parameters are important to maintain in reef aquaria.

A hobbyist's attention to water purity and the overall quality of synthetic salt mix are often rewarded with seldom-seen spectacles, such as these spawning lettuce slugs (Tridachia sp.).

parameters of the elements known to be important to all marine organisms. Some blends are so far from natural seawater concentrations that it speaks volumes of the resilience that many marine organisms show in captivity when presented with such foreign water chemistry. While they may be able to survive in these conditions, they are often not in the greatest of health over the long term and because of this the hobbyist may have greater difficulty maintaining certain species than a fellow hobbyist maintaining a more accurate representation of natural seawater parameters.

Ideally, marine aquarium water should contain the major, minor, and trace elements in the proper ratios (i.e. the same ratios found in natural seawater). Although the majority of scenarios we will discuss throughout

Because the vast majority of marine aquarium hobbyists must establish, maintain, and balance the chemistry of seawater using products purchased off the shelf, a dilemma arises when they encounter the wall of salt mixes and chemical products at the local aquarium shop. The first thing a hobbyist must understand is the chemistry of the water in the aquarium; being well-versed on this topic will enable the aquarist to eliminate a large percentage of products from contention, based on the fact that the hobbyist will be able to read a label and determine whether or not the product is necessary for his or her aquarium. A basic guideline to follow when making a decision about which products will be added to marine aquaria is to read the label. Are the ingredients listed? Is there a guaranteed analysis? Are the directions understandable? Is the manufacturer's contact information provided? If possible, open two bottles of the same product and compare the colors or appearance of the liquid or powder. Are they the same? They should be.

this book will be associated with tropical coral reefs, it's interesting to note that the ratios of most elements present in seawater are essentially constant throughout the world's oceans. That being the case, aquaria housing organisms endemic to temperate latitudes will have chemical requirements similar to those in the tropics; the major difference between the systems is water temperature, which must be kept cooler in a temperate system than in a tropical one, often with the use of one or more chillers. Table 1 details what I consider to be the ideal, and most important, water parameters for tropical reef aquaria.

Water Parameters

With regards to water quality, maintaining a healthy and thriving aquarium is typically an all-or-nothing scenario, because allowing the concentration of even one water parameter to lie outside its acceptable limits for a prolonged period of time can often lead to disaster. Perhaps this is one of the reasons that many long-time freshwater aquarists are leery of

▲ *Arc-eye hawkfish,* Paracirrhites arcatus. *Water quality is no less important to the long-term health of fishes than it is to invertebrates.*

setting up a seawater system; in many freshwater systems, allowing the ammonia to creep up or chronically exist at a relatively low concentration is allowable (largely as a result of the relationship between ammonia/ammonium and pH), but this is not possible in most marine aquaria.

In reality, maintaining the correct levels of various parameters is quite easy. Regular water changes, using a high-quality synthetic salt mix (for most hobbyists that do not have access to filtered seawater) and the correct supplements and/or additives, and regular testing of the water with accurate test kits or analysis equipment are the three easiest and most effective means of ensuring that the water contains several important constituents at the correct levels while minimizing the levels of less desirable or toxic substances, such as phosphate, silicate, ammonia, nitrite, and nitrate. Even in a system outfitted with several thousand dollars' worth of filtration equipment, ultimately it's the aquarist that needs to make sure everything is working properly.

Controlling Waste

Increasing concentrations of waste substances and their by-products, both those excreted by marine animals and those exuded by plant life, are a very large concern in a closed marine aquarium system. In many cases, the desirable organisms aren't accustomed to being subjected to waste substances in even the lowest concentrations, because the ocean is a truly enormous ecosystem (covering roughly two-thirds of the

Earth's surface and containing 97 percent of the total water on the planet), and waste is quickly diluted into the massive volume of water and/or utilized as nutrient material by marine life. Just as in the ocean, the waste products in an aquarium are continually broken down and incorporated into the tissues of living organisms.

In addition to this mechanism of nutrient remineralization, from which we get biological filtration, aquarists employ means of exporting waste via mechanical and chemical filtration. The use of these three types of filtration in a closed marine aquarium system facilitates the removal of substances that, once they begin to approach dangerous concentrations, would otherwise become harmful to the inhabitants. Hence, a complete filtration system helps the inhabitants remain healthy, though such a system is only effective if it's capable of handling the waste produced by all of the organisms in the system, and only then if properly maintained. We will return to these points later. In the following sections, we will discuss the chemistry at work in a marine aquarium, and the roles that synthetic salt mixes, supplements, and water-treatment chemicals play.

CHAPTER 2

Characteristics of Natural and Synthetic Seawater

Due to the great importance of creating and maintaining a stable and proper chemical environment for captive marine organisms, the discussion of seawater and synthetic salt blends must be rather extensive. The information that follows will be of tremendous value, however, to hobbyists of all experience levels when taking into account important aspects of water quality and deciding which salt blend to purchase. A general discussion of the chemical characteristics of seawater is crucial to understanding why certain salt blends are more desirable than others.

Ion Soup

Seawater can be thought of as an ion soup, containing most of the naturally occurring elements on our planet. It is composed of major elements (present in concentrations of greater than 1 ppm of the total weight of the dissolved solids in the water), minor elements (present in concentrations of 1 ppb to 1 ppm), and trace elements (present in concentrations of less than 1 ppb). Some of the elements are affected by marine life and water chemistry and are said to exhibit non-conservative behavior; notable examples are carbon, nitrogen, phosphorus, and silicate. Elements that are not affected by biological or chemical processes are said to exhibit conservative behavior.

One might think that calcium would be classified as exhibiting non-conservative behavior, since it is used

▲ *This orange-spotted shrimp goby,* **Amblyeleotris guttata,** *is sitting on a pile of artificial live rock made of foamed ceramic. Such material is a viable alternative to other types of live rock for maintaining water quality; it is typically higher in overall surface area, is far lighter and therefore displaces less water, and is man-made, so it represents no impact on the environment.*

in great quantity by a variety of invertebrates for skeletal or shell manufacture. Calcium, however, is in a specialized category of elements known as biointermediate; this indicates that while many organisms extract calcium from the surrounding water, the concentration never depletes appreciably due to the constant supply of calcium provided largely by remineralization of calcareous particles that dissolve as they fall toward the deep ocean floor. This is why the concentration of calcium varies very little throughout the world's oceans.

The significance of making the distinction between conservative and non-conservative elements is apparent when looking at the overall composition of seawater in different geographical locations, and a reef aquarium is often a great example of a system that experiences serious chemical fluctuations on an ongoing basis. Calcium may be considered a great illustrator of this point. A small volume of water in which several calcium-extracting organisms are present (such as a reef aquarium) should (and does) experience a gradual depletion in the concentration of calcium. A reef hobbyist may choose to add a calcium chloride supplement to their system to maintain the calcium concentration within the desired range, and in doing so they increase the concentration of calcium and chloride ions. In this case, calcium behaves in a non-conservative fashion due to the lack of naturally occurring calcium sources in the aquarium, whereas chloride behaves conservatively. In short, calcium will continue to be depleted by the inhabitants, however the chloride concentration will continue to increase with each dose of the supplement. With each subsequent addition of the calcium chloride salt, the ratios of the ions in the water get further out of balance. It is largely for these reasons (biological depletion of various elements and supplementation of salts that increase the concentration of conservative elements) that regular water changes in a marine aquarium are absolutely necessary!

Nutrients

Many of the substances present in seawater may be considered nutrients, substances necessary for the growth of primary producers such as algae, phytoplankton, and plants; the availability of these

Fig. 2.1 Oceanic Elemental and Ionic Concentrations

Atomic #	Common Name	Element	Molecular Weight	ppm
1	Hydrogen	H (as H_2O)	1.00794	55,789.479
2	Helium	He	4.0026	7.385 x10^{-06}
3	Lithium	Li	6.941	1.779 x10^{-01}
4	Beryllium	Be	9.01218	6.004 x10^{-07}
5	Boron	B	10.81	4.654
6	Carbon	C (organic)	12.011	4.925 x10^{-02}
7	Nitrogen	N (as NO_3)	14.0067	4.307 x10^{-01}
8	Oxygen	O (gas)	15.9994	3.608
9	Fluorine	F	18.9984	1.324
10	Neon	Ne	20.179	1.551 x10^{-04}
11	Sodium	Na	22.9898	11,075.336
12	Magnesium	Mg	24.305	1,320.3691
13	Aluminum	Al	26.9815	8.297 x10^{-04}
14	Silicon	Si	28.055	2.876
15	Phosphorus	P	30.9738	7.302 x10^{-02}
16	Sulfur	S	32.06	920.122
17	Chlorine	Cl	35.453	19,986.629
18	Argon	Ar	39.948	6.142 x10^{-01}
19	Potassium	K	39.0983	408.773
20	Calcium	Ca	40.08	423.145
21	Scandium	Sc	44.9559	6.912 x10^{-07}
22	Titanium	Ti	47.88	9.815 x10^{-04}
23	Vanadium	V	50.9415	1.201 x10^{-03}

Fig. 2.1 Oceanic Elemental and Ionic Concentrations/continued

Atomic #	Common Name	Element	Molecular Weight	ppm
24	Chromium	Cr	51.996	2.132×10^{-04}
25	Manganese	Mn	54.938	2.816×10^{-04}
26	Iron	Fe	55.847	5.724×10^{-05}
27	Cobalt	Co	58.9332	1.812×10^{-06}
28	Nickel	Ni	58.69	4.813×10^{-04}
29	Copper	Cu	63.546	2.605×10^{-04}
30	Zinc	Zn	65.39	4.021×10^{-04}
31	Galium	Ga	69.72	2.144×10^{-05}
32	Germanium	Ge	72.59	5.208×10^{-06}
33	Arsenic	As	74.9216	1.766×10^{-03}
34	Selenium	Se	78.96	1.376×10^{-04}
35	Bromine	Br	79.904	68.797
36	Krypton	Kr	83.8	2.920×10^{-04}
37	Rubidium	Rb	85.4678	1.226×10^{-01}
38	Strontium	Sr	87.62	7.814
39	Yttrium	Y	88.9059	1.367×10^{-05}
40	Zirconium	Zr	91.225	2.805×10^{-05}
41	Niobium	Nb	92.9064	4.761×10^{-06}
42	Molybdenum	Mo	95.94	1.082×10^{-02}
43	Technetium	Tc	98	Not Detected
44	Ruthenium	Ru	101.07	Not Detected
45	Rhodium	Rh	102.906	Not Detected
46	Paladium	Pd	106.42	Not Detected

Fig. 2.1 Oceanic Elemental and Ionic Concentrations/continued

Atomic #	Common Name	Element	Molecular Weight	ppm
47	Silver	Ag	107.868	2.764×10^{-06}
48	Cadmium	Cd	112.41	8.065×10^{-05}
49	Indium	In	114.82	1.177×10^{-07}
50	Tin	Sn	118.71	4.867×10^{-07}
51	Antimony	Sb	121.75	1.498×10^{-04}
52	Tellurium	Te	127.6	Not Detected
53	Iodine	I	126.905	5.723×10^{-02}
54	Xenon	Xe	131.29	6.729×10^{-05}
55	Cesium	Cs	132.905	2.997×10^{-04}
56	Barium	Ba	137.33	1.408×10^{-02}
57	Lanthanum	La	138.906	4.271×10^{-06}

substances limits biological production. Silicate, phosphorus (as phosphate), nitrogen (as nitrate and ammonium), and carbon (obtained from the decomposition of organic material) all have an impact on the appearance of a marine aquarium. Given that the abundance of carbon doesn't limit primary production, it is generally not considered a nutrient, but rather a bio-intermediate constituent. The concentration of nutrients is so important to the proper balance of a reef aquarium that it is completely realistic to see limited growth and uptake of calcium and other elements incorporated into the skeletal mass of reef-building organisms when nutrients are stripped from the water. We will explore this matter in detail when we discuss the roles that nitrogen, phosphorus, and organic matter play in a balanced marine environment.

Gases

Some of the elements found in seawater are present in the form of dissolved gases, the most notable of which being oxygen. While oxygen is present at a concentration of 3.5 ppm in seawater, it's typically not included in a list of major elements due to its gaseous state; silica and nitrogen, which are nutrients, are also sometimes excluded from this list due to their non-conservative nature and inconsistent concentrations in natural seawater.

Other dissolved gases present in seawater are nitrous oxide, carbon monoxide, methane, methyl iodide, and dimethyl sulphide. All are largely the result of biological processes that occur in sediments and again are of relatively minor importance to the average marine aquarium hobbyist.

Creating Seawater

Figure 2.1 lists the mean concentrations of each element observed in natural seawater. Some elements may be present in concentrations so small that modern analytical methods aren't refined enough to detect them.

A successful marine aquarium begins with quality seawater, which is more often than not synthetic in nature (owing to the difficulty and expense involved with obtaining natural seawater free of contaminants and elevated concentrations of nutrients). Several brands of marine salt mixes are available to aquarists, and the debate over which one is best is a source of on-going controversy in the marine aquarium hobby. To make some sense of the matter, we must discuss the properties generally acknowledged as belonging to a superior (or even an adequate) salt blend; from that information it will be simpler to identify which salts are best suited to the needs of your particular system.

Quality Salt Blends

A quality salt blend should provide all the major and minor ions listed in Figure 2.1 in the correct proportions, with a few key exceptions that we will discuss briefly. Without having a

Though the pajama cardinalfish, Sphaeramia nematoptera, *is known for being tolerant of wide-ranging water parameters, it will not look its best under suboptimal conditions. All marine aquaria are relatively delicate ecosystems, completely dependent upon the dedication of the hobbyist to creating and maintaining an environment that will support livestock, and water quality starts with the proper chemical composition.* ▶

comprehensive analysis performed on the salt (which requires the use of expensive laboratory equipment such as an inductively coupled plasma atomic-emission spectrometer, or ICP-AES), determining whether or not all of the crucial criteria are met is practically impossible; unfortunately, the time and money involved with performing such an accurate analysis are prohibitive to most hobbyists.

Even if the analysis *can* be performed, there's a chance that the package tested may not be representative of the majority of batches produced by the manufacturer, requiring multiple tests on product from multiple batches, with one end result being a rather large bill from the testing facility. There are a few analyses published on the Internet that were alledgedly performed by independent, impartial chemical companies and professionals, however some of these have since been discovered to be marketing ploys to discredit competing salt manufacturers. If you seek accurate information about the ingredients and their respective concentrations in a salt, contact the manufacturer for information; reputable manufacturers will be more than happy to spend some time with you, either on the phone, via e-mail, or in person at stores and seminars, and answer your questions about their products. They should be willing to provide you with an assay of the salt, either verbally or by e-mailing or faxing you an average analysis. If you contact a manufacturer about their salt and they are unable (or simply refuse) to provide you with information about the major components of their product or the elements that are present, it is a strong indication to use another brand.

Keep in mind that there's a limit to the information a manufacturer can provide on the chemical composition of a product, due to proprietary formulas that are sought after by competitors; unwillingness or inability to answer certain specific questions does not necessarily indicate any flaw in the manufacturer or their product, it may simply be considered confidential information. In other words, don't expect to get the formula for the salt from the manufacturer, but do expect to get the average concentrations of such ions as calcium, magnesium, carbonates, sodium, chloride, sulfate, and potassium. These are the most prevalent ions in seawater, and unwillingness or inability of the manufacturer to provide the average concentration that a hobbyist can expect to obtain when preparing a sample of water to a standard salinity raises a question as to the overall quality of the product or the manufacturing practices utilized; these are grounds to seek an alternate brand of salt.

Ideally, a manufacturer of synthetic sea salt would be able to provide information on the concentrations of most, if not all, major and minor ions in its mix when the salt is blended to a given salinity with purified water; in addition to the aforementioned ions, these (and other parameters) include, but are not limited to, disclosing concentrations of strontium, iron, iodine, phosphate, silicate, and nitrate, presence of trace elements, and the average pH and alkalinity obtained at that salinity.

Salt Processing

A final consideration is the method in which the salt is processed; the highest quality mixes are obtained by blending precise amounts of high-purity ingredients in a clean and arid environment using stainless steel machinery. This is the exception, not the norm, with many salt blends, so the hobbyist has their work in choosing a quality product cut out for them.

Salt that is obtained through evaporation of seawater is undesirable for two main reasons. First, although the seawater may be filtered before the water is evaporated, plankton and other life forms in the water that die during the collection process result in elevated concentrations of dissolved organic matter in the salt mix, which can have a negative impact on the aquarium as

The coloration, general appearance, and reproductive success of aquarium inhabitants are directly affected by the quality of the water they reside in. These and other zoanthids have consistently reproduced both asexually and sexually since their introduction to this well-balanced system.

time progresses. Second, as the salt dries, the constituent ions react with each other and form a number of salts that are highly insoluble under normal aquarium conditions (causing depressed concentrations of calcium, carbonate, and sulfate), which in short means that the water cannot reconstitute to the original solution.

A salt mix should be as dry as possible, as water present in the mix tends to act as a transport mechanism by which salts undergo reactions to form largely insoluble, and therefore largely useless, compounds during the interim between the production of the salt and its final use. Salts that are shipped in a semi-wet or moist form, or are hard as a brick (indicating that moisture has penetrated the bag, box, or bucket and has caused the salt to solidify) should be avoided. One of the factors that dictate the final retail price of a salt blend is its weight (specifically as it pertains to shipping costs, regardless of where the product is purchased), and it's probably safe to say that you don't want to pay for the weight of water in a salt mix. A quality salt mix should be free-flowing and homogenous in appearance.

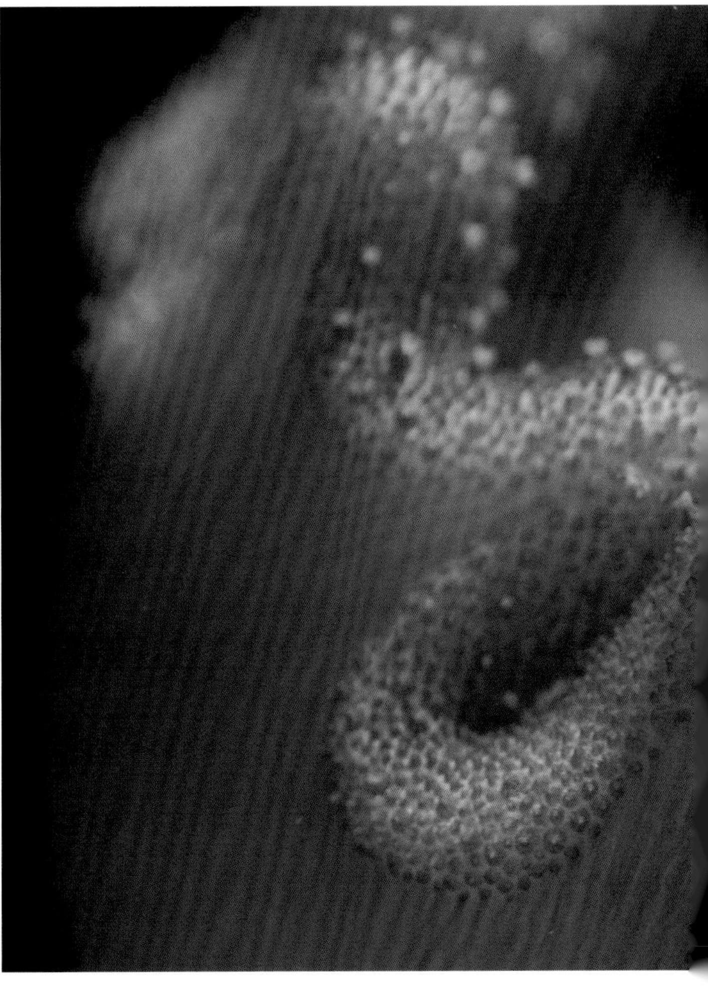

Be aware that there are salt mixes available containing higher than suggested concentrations of trace elements such as arsenic and copper. Many of these are a result of contaminants present in even the highest grades of raw materials used in the production of the salt. A good general rule to remember is that a premium salt blend commands a premium price due to the cost of high-purity raw materials, quantities used, extensiveness of the ingredient list, amortization of equipment utilized in the production of the salt blend, and skill level of the production personnel. Inexpensive salt blends are

The coloration, general appearance, and reproductive success of aquarium inhabitants are directly affected by the quality of the water they reside in.

often relatively cheap because the manufacturers place different priorities on these aspects of their product quality.

Choosing a Salt Mix

A large part of deciding which salt blend to use as a staple may come from accounts of other hobbyists. It is strongly encouraged that hobbyists rely largely on their own observations formulated over a period of months before making a decision to love or hate a specific salt blend, or any other product for that matter, and to seek the advice of other experienced hobbyists in aquarium societies or knowledgeable retail professionals as support for their decisions. Specific questions pertaining to a product should be addressed with the manufacturer as often as possible, for these are the people that should be able to answer all questions pertaining to the product itself and the impact that it's likely to have on any given aquarium system.

Mixing the Salt and Water

Preparing artificial seawater is quite simple: dissolve approximately 4 oz., or half a cup, of salt mix in each gallon of (preferably) purified water to obtain a target specific gravity between 1.021 and 1.026 g/cm^3. Because of differences in the formulas of the various salt mixes and the percentages of hydrated salts used, different ratios of salt to water are needed to obtain a standard specific gravity. Water purified via reverse osmosis and/or deionization should be used for preparation of artificial seawater. Some hobbyists may notice a bit of a paradox in this water-mixing scenario: if a specific amount of salt is added to a specific amount of water, shouldn't the resultant salinity be the same for every synthetic salt mix available? Not necessarily. The catch is that chemicals are available to manufacturers in many forms, some more pure than others, and some which are "hydrated," or bound with water molecules. So by weight, if a salt mix contains a large percentage of hydrated ingredients, it will dissolve to form a solution of lower specific gravity than a salt mix containing a lower percentage of these ingredients, all other aspects being equal.

Also, a salt mix that dissolves into a crystal clear solution within a few minutes' time, when compared to one that takes longer to clear, is not necessarily the superior product. It might be an indication that the blend has a much higher concentration of highly soluble salts, such as sodium chloride; it might be a result of the blending process; or (in the case of slow-mixing blends) it might simply be due to contamination with water prior to mixing the samples. Of course, some salt blends are superior to others in one or more important aspects, so aquarists must choose carefully.

The salt and water should be mixed with a submersible pump for not less than one hour in a clean, inert (preferably plastic) bucket or vat that serves no purpose other than to store freshly made seawater. The more water that is being mixed, the more time should be allowed for sufficient mixing, and/or the greater the rate of water circulation inside the vessel should be. Allowing the water to mix extensively enables gas formed during the salt dissolution to escape, gas which could otherwise affect the pH of the aquarium and irritate sensitive tissues of fishes and invertebrates. When the seawater is clear, the salinity, pH, and alkalinity should be tested and verified to be within the desired range of values. Temperature of the water should be adjusted to that of the aquarium before adding it to the system.

Evaporation

Due to the presence of various heat sources in the aquarium system (lighting, submersible pumps, etc.), water is constantly evaporating. The majority of the salt, however, is left behind in this process, causing the salinity of the water inside the aquarium to gradually increase. Because the goal is to keep salinity as constant as possible, fresh water must be added periodically either by manual means or by employing a dosing system of some sort. To complicate matters, there are also transports of salt *out* of the aquarium, slowing the gradual increase in salinity alluded to above. Salt spray created as bubbles break at the surface of the water is a minor, but constant, export of salt from the system; the magnitude of the issue becomes apparent a few weeks after start-up, when layers of dried salt are found in areas where water splashes. Additionally, protein skimmers gradually remove seawater during the waste collection process, causing salinity to fluctuate as seawater is removed and fresh water added. For

▲ *Every living thing in your aquarium, from massive fishes to tiny lettuce slugs, will depend on your careful attention to water chemistry every day for the rest of their lives.*

these reasons, it's recommended that salinity be checked every few days to ensure that it is always within an acceptable range.

Chemical Supplementation

One more topic that warrants discussion is the issue of maintaining natural seawater parameters in an aquarium and the use of chemical supplements. Fundamentally, it makes perfect sense to maintain the concentrations of all ions in solution at natural seawater values, but as we discussed, the use of currently available synthetic sea-salt mixes, over which hobbyists have no formulation control, makes this impossible. Still, the majority of premium salt mixes will provide a suitable environment for our aquarium inhabitants. If acceptable chemistry can be established, why then can't hobbyists simply perform frequent water changes to maintain the proper concentrations? They can, if they are diligent in their pursuit of this goal and change a substantial percentage of the water in the system every day. The ideal salt blend would present as close a representation to natural seawater concentrations of all major, minor, and trace elements as possible, and the larger the percentage of overall system volume that was changed on a weekly basis, the more natural the chemistry of the water would be to the inhabitants.

Because most hobbyists make water changes less than once per month, however, they are forced to turn to supplements in an attempt to maintain desired parameters. There are no appreciable savings of money in the use of one method versus the other. Seawater is rich in dissolved substances and livestock depletes these substances with time; therefore, maintaining proper water chemistry in a marine aquarium is more expensive than in a freshwater aquarium. When it comes to reef aquarium husbandry, one thing is for certain: the hobbyist who establishes an aquarium with an inexpensive synthetic salt blend lacking in adequate concentrations of non-conservative major and minor ions will wind up spending additional money on supplements to correct the deficiencies before any animals are introduced to the system; in this manner, purchasing an inexpensive salt blend saves no money in the long run, and creates work that is easily avoided by using a premium salt blend.

CHAPTER 3

Salinity

Salinity is a term that refers to the concentration of inorganic ions in solution in a liter of water. It was once common to express salinity as parts of dissolved inorganic ion per thousand parts water, or ppT, also denoted by the per mil symbol, ‰. (Now it is typical to express salinity without units, since it is a proportion, so one speaks of a salinity of 35 rather than of 35‰.) Salinity is measured with a device called a salinometer which determines electrical conductivity relative to a pre-determined standard. The concentrations of major ions in seawater are so high that the other conductive ions in solution have very little impact on the overall reading. On average, natural seawater is 35‰, or 3.5%, dissolved salts, over 99.9% of which is attributable to major elements, for reference. Salinometers are rarely, if ever, used by aquarium hobbyists, for while capable of high precision and accuracy, they also tend to be far more expensive than alternative methods of determining salinity that are sufficiently accurate for the successful husbandry of captive marine organisms.

Density

An alternate means of measuring salinity deals with density. This can be measured with a hydrometer, which measures density relative to that of fresh water, or a refractometer, which utilizes the bending of light through the water sample to determine its

Bartlett's anthias, Pseudanthias bartlettorum, *has a relatively poor record of survival in captivity, largely owing to the difficulty of providing suitable foods for these planktivores. Keeping them in a system that has optimal water conditions and in which they are not outcompeted for food or bullied helps make the transition to captivity smoother and more successful.*

density. The density of pure fresh water is 1.000 g/cm^3, while seawater has an average density of approximately 1.024 g/cm^3. This means that ocean water is about 1.024 times as dense as pure water. At 70°F, this density corresponds with 35‰. This comparison of density is commonly referred to as the specific gravity, which compares the density of a substance to the density of pure water.

Hydrometers

Two types of hydrometers are available to aquarium hobbyists: floating glass hydrometers, and vessel-type hydrometers with indicator arrows. Floating hydrometers are typically more accurate than plastic swing-arm hydrometers, which often vary quite considerably in accuracy. Because the density of water is a function of

its temperature, hydrometers can only give accurate readings if the water they are sampling is of the temperature to which they were calibrated; older glass hydrometers were often calibrated at temperatures cooler than those at which most hobbyists maintain a tropical marine aquarium, but newer models are often calibrated at roughly 77°F or thereabouts.

For true precision when measuring the salinity or specific gravity of seawater, it's hard to beat the results given by refractometers, many of which automatically compensate for water temperature. The trouble most hobbyists run into is the price tag attached to these pieces of equipment, though they are gradually becoming more affordable.

Remember that the ultimate goal is to maintain the salinity or specific gravity within the specified range, keeping that reading as stable as possible over a long period of time. Because stability of salinity is crucial, the accuracy of readings actually becomes secondary to some extent.

CHAPTER 4

pH and Alkalinity

The concepts of pH and alkalinity may be two of the most confused and misunderstood in all of chemistry. In reality, they are quite easy to explain. The formal definition of pH is the negative log of the hydrogen ion activity (-log $\{H^+\}$), which is a means of expressing the relative abundance of hydrogen ions compared to hydroxide ions in solution. A more simplified explanation is essentially that pH is a measurement of the concentration of free hydrogen ions (H^+) in solution relative to that of free hydroxide ions (OH^-), or even more simply stated, pH is a measurement of a substance's acidity.

pH

If the concentration of hydrogen ions is greater than that of hydroxide ions, the substance is termed acidic. If the converse is true, the substance is termed basic. If the concentrations are equal, the substance has a neutral pH, neither acidic nor basic. The corresponding scale for expressing the hydrogen ion concentration runs from 0 to 14. An acidic substance has a pH less than 7.0, a basic substance has a pH greater than 7.0, and a neutral substance has a pH of 7.0. The pH scale is logarithmic, which means that a change in value of one whole number is a tenfold increase or decrease in acidity from the original concentration. If the pH in a system

pH Peril

Significantly altering pH within the actual aquarium system can negatively impact and even kill the inhabitants, so always take care to adjust pH gradually.

changes by two whole numbers, the change in acidity is a hundredfold. For example, if the pH of a solution changes from 8.0 to 7.0, the solution has become 10 times more acidic; if the pH further drops to 6.0, the solution has become 100 times more acidic than the original. As with all water parameters, pH in a marine aquarium should remain generally stable, to within three-tenths of a point (i.e. between 8.1 and 8.4) at all times.

The average pH of ocean water is approximately 8.3. Depending on the amount of carbonates and buffers present in a given blend, many synthetic salt mixes will only raise the pH of the mixed seawater to 8.1. Adding a pH-boosting supplement may therefore be necessary to raise pH to the desired level, and it's highly recommended that this step be performed outside the aquarium, such as in the mixing vessel, once the salt has completely dissolved and the specific gravity is at the desired value.

At this point, the pH can be determined and adjustments may be made as necessary. As with salinity, hobbyists should be more concerned with the stability of the pH value in their aquaria rather than being determined to maintain these values within a range of 8.1 and 8.4; successful hobbyists have been consistently maintaining pH values as low as 7.9 and as high as 8.5 in their reef aquaria for years with no apparent negative impact to the inhabitants. The important point is to not allow the pH to reach these

Figure 4.1 Understanding the pH Scale.

pH	Condition	Solution
< 7.0	$[H^+] > [OH^-]$	Acidic
> 7.0	$[OH^-] > [H^+]$	Basic
= 7.0	$[H^+] = [OH^-]$	Neutral[1]

[1] This is only accurate at 77°F, or 25°C.

extremes on a daily basis, as this degree of fluctuation may be detrimental to the inhabitants if allowed to persist over an extended period of time, such as a few days or possibly weeks.

Figure 4.2 Alkalinity Conversions		
1 meq/L	=	50 mg $CaCO_3$/L
	=	2.8 dKH
1 mg $CaCO_3$/L	=	0.02 meq/L
	=	0.056 dKH
1 dKH	=	0.36 meq/L
	=	17.86 mg $CaCO_3$/L

Alkalinity

Alkalinity is the ability of a substance to resist a change in pH—in other words, the ability to maintain a stable pH. Substances that suppress a change in pH are largely known as buffering substances, or buffers for short, and may include carbonate (CO_3^{2-}), bicarbonate (HCO_3^-), borate ($B(OH)_4^-$), hydroxide (OH^-), silicate (SiO_3^{2-}), and phosphate (PO_4^{3-}). Of these, bicarbonate plays the most important role in the marine aquarium. Buffers react in solution with acids, such as carbonic acid produced by microbial decomposition of organic material and respiration by all aquarium residents, and help prevent the pH of the solution from lowering. This is very important for the continued health of the organisms in the system, whose ancestors have spent the past several million years evolving in an environment with a pH that has varied very little over short periods of time. Buffering substances are gradually depleted from the system as they react with acids, requiring their regular addition to an aquarium if pH is to remain stable. The controlled use of a buffering product and regular water changes with a salt containing adequate amounts of buffers will prevent this depletion.

Expressing Alkalinity

There are three methods of expressing alkalinity generally used in marine aquarium care: milligrams of calcium carbonate per liter water (mg $CaCO_3$/L), milliequivalents per liter (meq/L), and degrees of carbonate hardness (dKH, explained in the

▲ *Overfeeding, which can be a danger with picky eaters like sun polyps,* **Tubastraea sp.***, can be detrimental to water quality, increasing the concentration of dissolved and particulate organic material, lowering the redox potential, and lowering alkalinity and potentially pH.*

following chapter). Most alkalinity test kits will give results in at least one of these units. Figure 4.2 shows the relationships between these units of measurement.

As indicated in Table 1.1, the recommended alkalinity for marine aquarium systems is 2.5 to 3.6 meq/L, corresponding to approximately 7 to 10 dKH or 126 to 180 mg $CaCO_3$/L. By keeping the alkalinity of the system within the recommended range, pH should remain stable. Note that it's not wise to maintain alkalinity in great excess of the maximum

recommended value, as doing so can interfere with the ability of free calcium ions to remain in solution, in turn making it very difficult to maintain the residual calcium concentration within the desired range. Reef hobbyists should pay particular attention to this fact.

There is a relationship between calcium, magnesium, and strontium concentrations and alkalinity that many aquarists find very confusing. Corals and other reef-building organisms deposit varying amounts of minerals containing calcium, magnesium, strontium, and carbonates as skeletal material, enabling them to grow. The carbonates utilized in this process are largely removed from the surrounding water, which creates another need to buffer a reef system regularly; in the absence of adequate carbonates, not only would reef-building organisms be prevented from secreting a skeleton, but pH in the system would eventually begin to fall.

CHAPTER 5

General and "Carbonate" Hardness

Although this topic may be better suited to discussion in a book dealing with chemistry in freshwater aquaria, it's very important that marine aquarium hobbyists develop a solid understanding of the reasons that so-called general and carbonate hardness (abbreviated GH and KH, respectively) are not the same, for this is a common misconception among beginning hobbyists. The misunderstanding may be largely due to the fact that so many explanations on the differences between these parameters exist in literature.

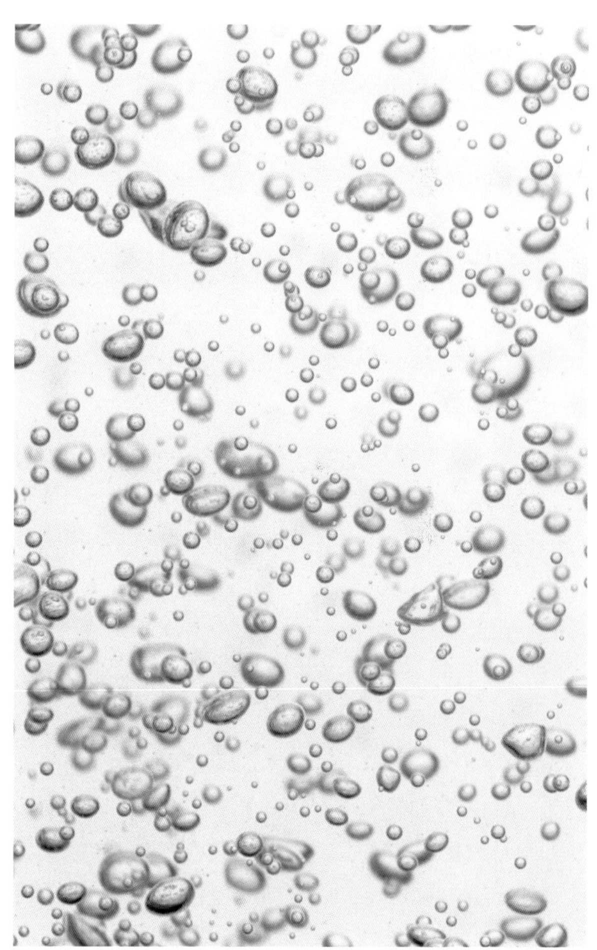

General Hardness

GH is not an abbreviation for "general hardness;" rather, it is an abbreviation

◀ *Marine fishes, such as this blackcap gramma,* Gramma malecara, *can often tolerate pH fluctuations of greater magnitude than many hobbyists imagine, but it is unwise to "push the envelope." Maintaining carbonate hardness at the minimum recommended value will minimize pH shift and provide a more stable and hospitable environment for aquatic organisms.*

for *Gesamthaerte*, German for "total hardness." In spite of this, it may be simpler to think of GH as "general hardness" (owing to the frequency with which the term is found throughout aquarium literature), as long as the true definition of the term is adhered to. GH is defined as the sum of divalent cations in solution (ions with a charge of $^{+2}$), including such elements as calcium, magnesium, strontium, and many species of heavier metals such as iron and copper. Because magnesium and calcium ions are vastly more abundant in water than other divalent cation species, GH is essentially the combined concentration of magnesium and calcium ions. Note that it does not encompass the concentrations of monovalent (having a charge of $^{+/-1}$) cations or anions in solution, such as sodium and chloride which make up over 85 percent of dissolved substances in seawater (and a large percentage in fresh water, for that matter).

"Carbonate" Hardness

KH, or *Karbonathaerte*, is a measurement of alkalinity of the solution. Often misleadingly termed "carbonate hardness" in the aquarium hobby, alkalinity is essentially a

Testing General Hardness

A few GH test kits are able to distinguish the calcium concentration from other divalent cations present in a sample. This makes it possible to get a rough estimate of the magnesium concentration in solution—subtracting the calcium concentration from the measured GH leaves the magnesium concentration. This is good information to have on hand if the local aquarium shop doesn't stock a magnesium test kit. The only drawback to the accuracy of these test kits is that the calcium measurement often includes the strontium concentration in the sample, so a truly accurate calcium reading isn't possible unless the strontium concentration in the aquarium is already known.

measurement of the concentration of the anions carbonate, hydroxide, phosphate, silicate, and borate in solution. In seawater, alkalinity comes mainly from carbonate and bicarbonate liberated during dissociation from various cations. Carbonate hardness is said to be "temporary" hardness because the liberated carbonates react so quickly with acids present in the sample; once that happens, the alkalinity is depleted.

Taking all this information into consideration, it should be apparent that GH and KH are not measuring the same parameters. While GH takes into account Mg^{2+} and Ca^{2+}, KH measures carbonates largely derived from Na_2CO_3 and $NaHCO_3$. It is also prudent to mention that GH and total dissolved solids (TDS) are not different ways of measuring the same parameter. A TDS meter measures the sum of *electrically charged* substances in solution, expressed in units of ppm. Now, it can *generally* be said that a solution with high GH will have high TDS, but a solution with high TDS won't necessarily have high GH (remember that TDS takes *all ions* into account, such as sodium and chloride, and GH does not). The subject of TDS is discussed at greater length in the chapter detailing water purification.

CHAPTER 6

Dissolved Oxygen

Concentrations of dissolved oxygen (DO) gas are very important to aerobic (oxygen-breathing) aquatic organisms, but maintaining the minimum required concentration of DO can sometimes be a challenge in marine aquaria. There are two main reasons for this. Gas solubility is inversely related to the density of a liquid, meaning that the higher the liquid's density, the lower the amount of gas that can be dissolved in it, and gas solubility in liquid is inversely related to water temperature. Because seawater is denser than fresh, and because the temperature of marine aquarium water is typically greater than 75°F, the volume of gas able to exist in the water is relatively low.

Like many marine fishes, the half-black angelfish, Centropyge vroliki, *is relatively intolerant of low dissolved-oxygen (DO) levels. Higher salinity and water temperature limit the concentration of attainable DO, so adequate circulation at the air-water interface must be provided to encourage gas exchange and hence oxygenation of the aquarium water.*

The Importance of Oxygen

So-called "ornamental" aquatic organisms (that is, those that are commonly kept in aquaria) are largely unable to deal with extended periods of low-oxygen conditions without serious risk of death. Therefore, it is crucial that the hobbyist ensure sufficient means of oxygenating the water on a continuous basis. The saturation point of dissolved oxygen in seawater is approximately 8 mg/L. If that concentration drops below 5 mg/L, large fishes and invertebrates begin to appear stressed, and can usually be seen hovering near the air-

water interface at the surface, where the concentration of dissolved oxygen is greatest—that is, if the organism in question is capable of moving itself near the aquarium water surface. In the event of oxygen depletion in the system, invertebrates will typically die before fishes.

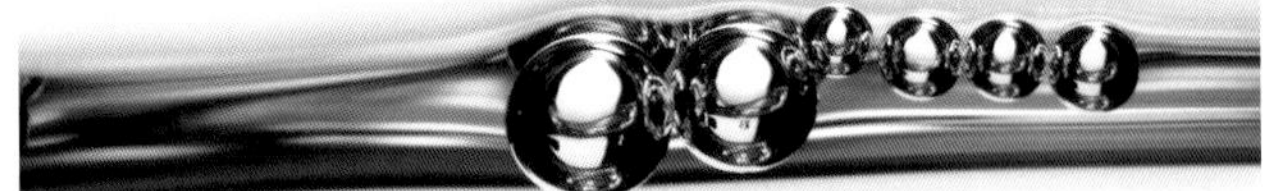

The Dangers of Oxygen Depletion

If oxygen depletion is not noticed early and stopped before organisms begin to die, the situation may deteriorate very rapidly. The typical progression is:

- *Aerobic bacteria, such as those responsible for reducing ammonia and nitrite, quickly die in the absence of sufficient oxygen, such as during a power outage or a long-term interruption in the agitation of water at the aquarium surface.*
- *The dead bacteria begin to decompose, causing the concentration of DO in the water to further deplete. In a system with a large bacterial population, such as that found in aquaria with a deep substrate, the entire aerobic bacteria population can die within a few hours.*
- *Fishes and invertebrates begin to perish as they suffocate in the low-oxygen environment.*

A somewhat common situation in which this process can occur is during extensive aquarium maintenance and the interruption of the main aquarium pumps. The use of multiple powerheads at the water's surface will typically create enough circulation and gas exchange to inject oxygen from the overlying air into the aquarium to maintain a stable system. However, steps must be taken to ensure that the currents are directed across the surface of the water and not below it. If a powerhead somehow becomes detached from the side of the aquarium or the exhaust port moves such that the current is no longer causing surface agitation, the result (if not corrected within a matter of several minutes) can be an aquarium full of suffocated organisms.

Factors that affect the amount of time in which the surface agitation must be re-established are surface area of the aquarium, the specific gravity and temperature of the water, and the biological oxygen demand (which is determined by the stocking density

and size of organisms in the aquarium, mass and porosity of live rock, and depth and average particle size of the sand bed, if one is employed in the aquarium). As surface area decreases and the remaining criteria increase, the amount of time available to implement surface agitation or some other means of oxygen injection decreases.

Oxygenating the Aquarium

Maximizing the amount of DO in the system can be easily achieved with rigorous water movement, especially at the air-water interface (i.e. surface of the water). Wave-makers are very useful in this regard; they produce variable currents for short periods of time that churn the water and inject oxygen into the system. Vigorous aeration of the water with an air pump and air stone promotes oxygenation; however, a disadvantage to using this method is that it creates salt spray, which is unsightly and impacts the salinity of the system as discussed previously. Another effective means of injecting oxygen into aquarium water is to pass water over a column of suspended biological media in a sump beneath the main aquarium. As water crashes down over the media, air mixes in while other gases, such as carbon dioxide and nitrogen, are driven out. Lastly, maintaining macroalgae in a refugium that is illuminated on an opposite schedule to the main aquarium lighting encourages oxygenation and the uptake of carbon dioxide on a continuous basis. Many of these points are discussed at greater length in subsequent chapters.

CHAPTER 7

The Marine Nitrogen Cycle

The metabolic processes of animals and decomposition of organic matter (such as uneaten food and dead plant material) create several by-products, one of which is particulate organic nitrogen. This is broken down (remineralized) into dissolved organic nitrogen, which in turn is broken down (ammonified) into ammonia gas (NH_3). Ammonia is a molecule similar in some respects to water, but it is toxic to fishes and invertebrates in relatively small concentrations due to its interference with oxygen transport from the gills. Because it's so rapidly broken down by bacteria and taken up by primary producers in the wild, marine organisms have had little need to evolve a tolerance to high concentrations of ammonia.

The ocean comprises an enormous volume of water, and is home to countless organisms that convert ammonia into forms that are progressively less toxic to marine life. This series of oxidation and reduction reactions comprises the **marine nitrogen cycle**. In the open water of reef ecosystems (above the reef itself), the concentration of ammonia in the water is so low it cannot be measured. It is often higher in the sediments of areas of high run-off near coastlines, such as estuaries, where a profusion of organic matter is entering the ocean and settling out of suspension. Organisms endemic to areas such as these may be able to tolerate low concentrations of ammonia. On the other hand, since fresh water typically has a lower pH

▲ *Tridacnid clams, such as this* Tridacna squamosa, *may be employed as a sink for nitrate in reef aquaria, but any appreciable difference in the concentration of nitrate is likely to be noticed only if these clams are present at sufficient population densities relative to the available nutrients.*

than ocean water, a percentage of the ammonia in the run-off may be present as **ammonium** (NH_4^+), which exists not as a gas but as an ion. The significance of this ionized form is that a gas can be easily transported directly across a fish's gills and into the bloodstream, whereas an ion is not so easily transported in this manner. A concentration of approximately 0.02 mg/L ammonia appears to cause stress to fish, wheras the ammonium concentration may reach much higher concentrations before it begins to affect aquatic organisms.

Ammonia dissolved in water will obtain an extra hydrogen ion from water molecules themselves, and attains equilibrium as per Eq. 7.1.

(Eq. 7.1)

$$H_2O_{(l)} + NH_{3(aq)} \leftrightarrow NH_4^+{}_{(aq)} + OH^-{}_{(aq)}$$

Again, the abundance of the particular species of ammonia present, hence the overall toxicity of the molecule, is related to the pH of the water. The higher the pH, the more toxic ammonia there is, compared to relatively harmless ammonium; ammonium is more prevalent at lower pH. Using this information, the manner in which pH influences the percentage of toxic ammonia in a system is easily illustrated. The percentage of total ammonia present in the gaseous state is also influenced by water temperature; this is a result of the principle of chemistry that *equilibrium reactions tend to be temperature-dependent*. In summary, the ratio of ammonia and ammonium is dependent upon the pH and temperature of the solution—the higher the pH and/or temperature, the greater the ratio of ammonia to ammonium. Figure 7.1 shows the percentage of total ammonia (the sum of ammonia and ammonium) in solution as it relates to pH and temperature.

To use Figure 7.1 properly, obtain the total ammonia concentration in the aquarium and multiply it by the percentage that corresponds nearest to the pH and temperature of the water. If, for example, the total ammonia concentration measured is 1 mg/L, the water temperature is 79°F, and the pH is 8.3, then the total concentration of toxic ammonia in the aquarium is approximately 0.11 mg/L (1 x 11.0%). (To put things in perspective, at a pH of 7.0 the

Figure 7.1. Approximate Percentage of Toxic Ammonia Present in Solution with Varying pH and Temperature. pH is along y-axis, temperature (°F) is along x-axis.

pH/temp	75.0°F	77.0°F	79.0°F	81.0°F	83.0°F
8.0	5.0	5.4	5.7	6.1	6.5
8.1	6.4	6.8	7.3	7.8	8.3
8.2	7.7	8.3	8.8	9.4	10.0
8.3	9.7	10.4	11.0	11.7	12.5
8.4	11.7	12.5	13.3	14.1	15.0
8.5	14.5	15.5	16.4	17.4	18.4
8.6	17.4	18.4	19.5	20.6	21.8

corresponding concentration of toxic ammonia at this temperature would be only approximately 0.006 mg/L—20 times less). While inhabitants may weather short-term spikes in the ammonia concentration, they will not handle long-term exposure to elevated ammonia concentrations nearly as well. Remember to maintain the maximum concentration of ammonia below 0.02 mg/L as a rule to avoid killing aquarium inhabitants.

Nitrification

Ammonia (as the ammonium ion[1]) is principally removed from an aquarium by a host of nitrifying bacteria in part one of the two-step process of **nitrification**. The ammonium is oxidized to **nitrite** (NO_2^-) by the bacteria, causing the concentration of ammonium in the system to decline while the concentration of nitrite increases; this step in the nitrification process occurs very quickly, and therefore the concentration of ammonia/ammonium in open ocean water is essentially too tiny to be measured. Nitrite is nearly as toxic to aquatic organisms as ammonia, and therefore should be maintained at an

[1] The principal reason that the ammonia is taken up as ammonium is because of the difference in phase: ammonia is a gas while ammonium is an ion. Ions are more readily utilized by aquatic organisms than molecules in gaseous state. The means in which ammonia becomes ammonium is via reaction with hydrogen ions or water itself.

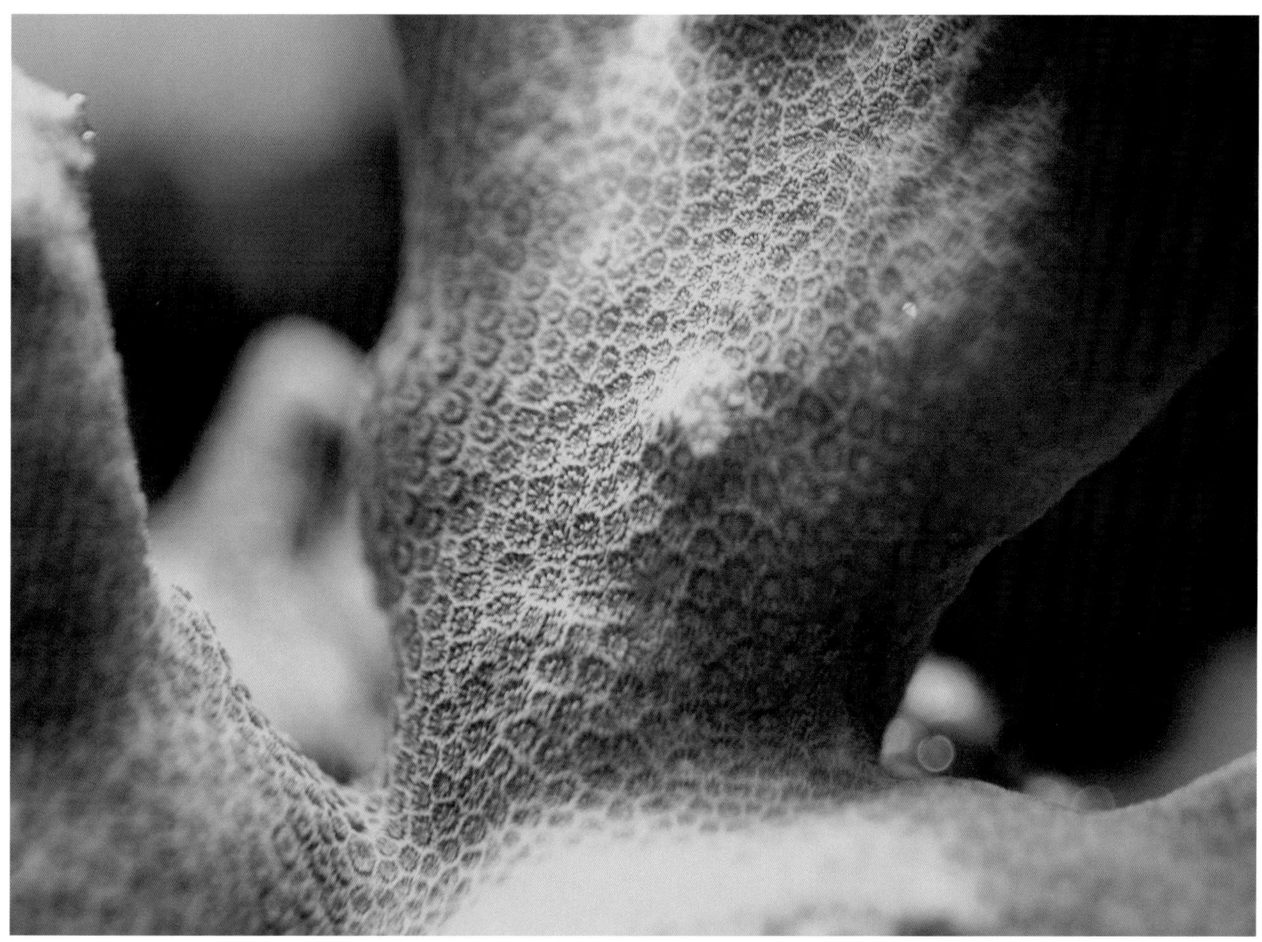

▲ *Balanced conditions, in which the concentrations of ammonia, nitrite, and nitrate are immeasurable, are optimal for the health of aquarium inhabitants like this Porites coral.*

immeasurable concentration at all times. This is easily accomplished in a system with a mature biological filter. The concentration of nitrite in the system will not reach such low levels until the bacteria responsible for nitrite oxidation have had time to reach the required population density and nitrification potential. As the concentration of nitrite increases in the system, a second suite of nitrifying bacteria oxidize the nitrite into **nitrate** (NO_3^-). In this step, the concentration of nitrite decreases as the concentration of nitrate increases. Again, this is a very rapid step in the nitrification process and the resulting concentration of nitrite in seawater is nearly nil.

Both of these reactions happen only in the presence of oxygen, a point that has great significance with respect to the nature of the media that the bacteria colonize and the environment in which they are maintained; details surrounding this requirement are addressed below and in the section dealing with aquarium filtration.

It is prudent to mention that with each additional organism added to the system (i.e. fishes or invertebrates), the amount of waste production per unit time and aquarium volume increases, which must be countered by an increase in the population density of nitrifying bacteria. It is for this reason that heavy stocking of a newly-established aquarium system often results in disaster. In a new system seeded with a few bacteria, such as those present in a handful of gravel taken from an established marine aquarium, it may take several weeks for the bacterial population to reach the required density and decrease the nitrite concentration sufficiently for the safety of ornamental aquarium inhabitants. On the other hand, using a complete external biological filter from an older, established system can often cycle an aquarium in a few days, depending on the capacity of the filter related to the overall biological load presented by the system.

Nitrate

Nitrate is one of the major nutrients in seawater. Its presence in a high concentration generally has more of an impact on the appearance of an aquarium than on the livestock—high concentrations of nitrate can encourage prolific growth of filamentous algae if no macroalgae are present in the system. Because of this, it is recommended that the nitrate concentration in an aquarium be maintained as low as possible.

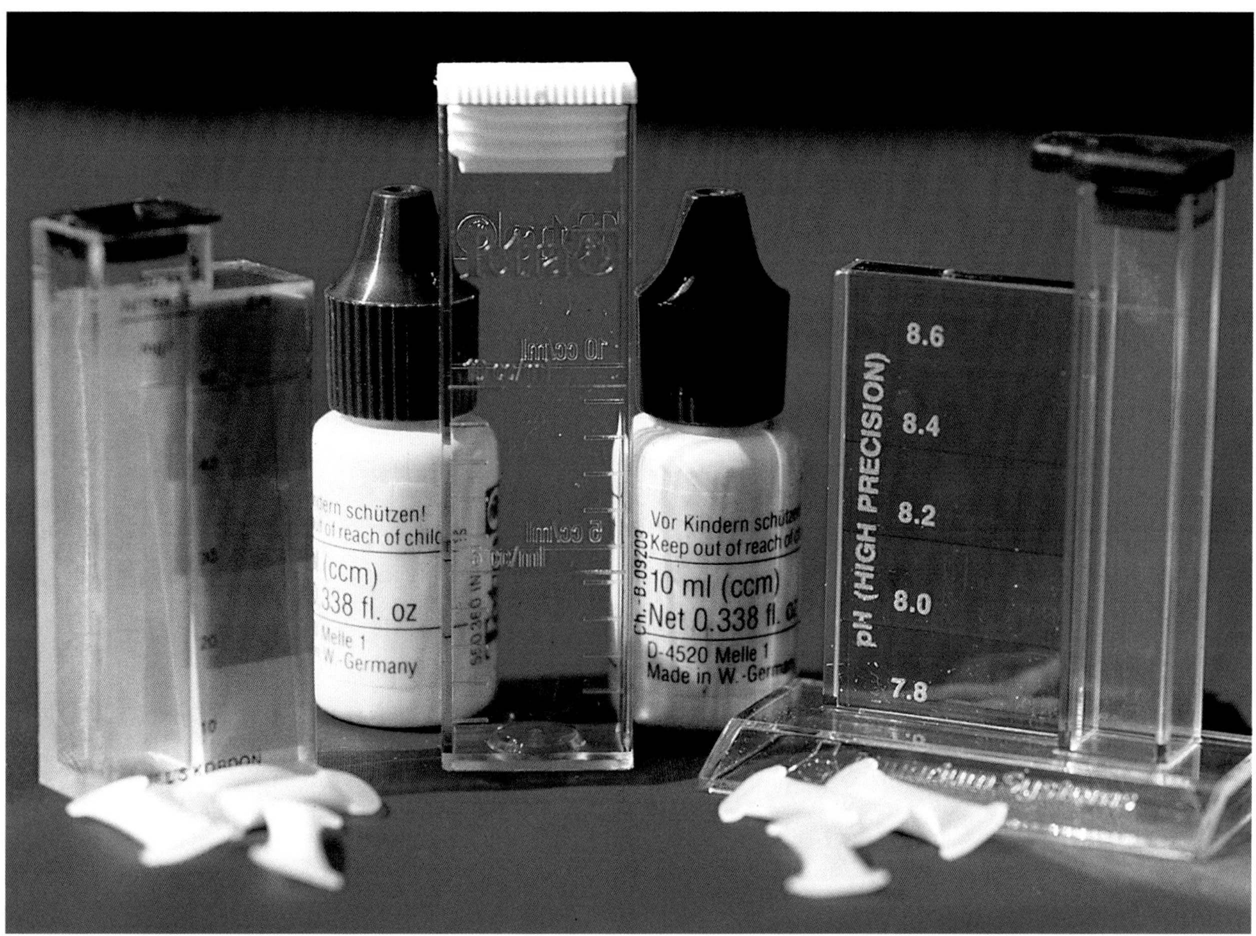

▲ ***Regular testing for ammonia, nitrite, and nitrate using accurate test kits should be part of every successful hobbyist's regimen.***

Nitrate concentrations in natural seawater are low to immeasurable, averaging 0.42 mg/L. There is some speculation that nitrate is toxic to marine invertebrates at a concentration greater than approximately 20 mg/L, and given that very little nitrate exists in seawater one could draw the conclusion that this toxicity is at least partially related to the fact that marine organisms have not had to develop a tolerance to this molecule. Fish-only aquaria seem to have relatively little trouble with elevated nitrate concentration, so long as the increase is very gradual[2], however continued health of the fish is more likely if the nitrate concentration is not allowed to exceed 50 mg/L at any time.

Denitrification

Denitrification is the process by which bacteria reduce nitrate back into nitrite, and then reduce the nitrite to nitrogen gas. This process occurs only in water that is undersaturated with oxygen, such as within nitrate-reduction filters or deep within live rock and beds of live sand (due to the removal of oxygen from water by the nitrifying bacteria occupying the layers nearer to the water), and requires some form of organic material as a source of food. These requirements are met by the gradual dispersion of dissolved and particulate organic material into the spaces between sand grains, the pores of live rock, or by direct addition to denitrification filters. As depth of the live sand bed or distance into the core of the rock or filter increases, the oxygen and nitrate concentrations in the water are decreased and increased, respectively, by aerobic nitrifying bacteria. The conditions for nitrate reduction are then established and the denitrification process takes place, with the bacteria utilizing latent organic material as a food source and nitrate as their electron acceptor.

(Eq. 7.2)

$$\mathbf{(CH_2O)_{106}(NH_3)_{16}H_3O_4 + 84.8\ HNO_3 \leftrightarrow 148.8\ H_2O + 106\ CO_2 + 42.4\ N_2 + 16\ NH_3 + H_3PO_4}$$

Eq. 7.2 illustrates that there are several products of the denitrification process (aside from water), all of which become utilized in some chemical or biological process: carbon dioxide eventually becomes part of the carbonate system, ammonia is transformed into ammonium, which further feeds the nitrification process, phosphoric acid is utilized by organisms capable of fixing it into biomass, and the nitrogen gas either escapes from the

[2] Nitrate has been recorded in concentrations of several hundred parts per million in public aquaria, gradually increasing with time. Ironically, large-scale water changes with nitrate-free water in these systems actually caused numerous fish mortalities as the nitrate concentration in the system was decreased too rapidly!

water into the atmosphere or is fixed by cyanobacteria (also called blue-green algae or sometimes "slime algae" by hobbyists). The ability of cyanobacteria to fix this nitrogen has special significance to hobbyists maintaining aquaria with deep sand beds and plenums, as we will discuss later on.

It typically takes some time for an aquarium to attain a consistent immeasurable nitrate concentration. An established reef system that is sensibly stocked, contains ample live rock and live sand, and in which influx of organic material is limited, usually has no measurable nitrate after six months of operation. Note that some aquarium systems may never reach this point because nitrate is produced faster than denitrifying bacteria are able to reduce it. This is most often due to the use of water or

◀ ***Carefully stocked and maintained reef aquaria can start to exhibit consistently immeasurable nitrate levels after about six months.***

A deep sand bed composed of too fine coverage particle size can be detrimental to aquarium inhabitants. This yellow-headed jawfish (Opistognathus aquifrons)*, however, will benefit from such a bed by being allowed to construct a burrow just as it would in the wild.*

salt that contains nitrate or as a result of overfeeding. Some hobbyists may rely solely on regular water changes to keep the persistent concentration of nitrate in check; others may choose to employ a system of filtration that facilitates the denitrification process.

Live Sand

Briefly addressing live sand in the context of nitrification and denitrification, two key questions arise: what should the average particle size of the sand be, and how deep should the bed be? First, it is prudent to clarify that "sand" is not a reference to silica-based beach sand or sandbox sand, but rather to aragonite particles, which we will refer to as "substrate." For the purpose of avoiding a build-up of organics in the substrate bed, it can

Figure 7.2. Substrate Depth Recommendations

Average Particle Diameter	Recommended Depth of Substrate
< 2 mm	1.0 to 2.0″ (2.5 to 5.0 cm)
2 to 4 mm	2.0 to 3.0″ (5.0 to 7.5 cm)
> 4 mm	3.0 to 6.0″ (7.5 to 15.0 cm)

generally be stated that the maximum desirable depth of the substrate is inversely related to the average size of the aragonite particles; in other words, the larger the average particle size, the deeper the substrate can be, while smaller average particle size requires shallower substrates. Larger particles have larger interstices, and water flows more readily through the bed. Because water is stripped of oxygen by aerobic bacteria and infauna as it flows down through the substrate, it becomes anoxic with increasing depth. When the nitrate concentration in the water is spent, bacteria will begin reducing sulfate obtained from organic material, ultimately forming hydrogen sulfide (H_2S), a poisonous gas that even in relatively low concentrations is capable of killing fishes and invertebrates. Equation 7.3 illustrates the process of sulfate reduction.

(Eq. 7.3)

$$(CH_2O)_{106}(NH_3)_{16}H_3PO_4 + 53\ SO_4^{2-} \rightarrow 106\ CO_2 + 106\ H_2O + 16\ NH_3 + 53\ S^{2-} + H_3PO_4$$

To avoid sulfate reduction in the substrate, follow the recommendations outlined in Figure 7.2

Depending on the rate at which the concentration of nitrate is increasing, water changes may need to be performed every week to two weeks. In essence, this equates to simple dilution as nitrate-laden water is removed from the system and replaced with nitrate-free water.

CHAPTER 8

Calcium and Carbonates

At an average concentration of approximately 412 mg/L, **calcium** is one of the major ions in seawater, present as Ca^{2+} and as a component of numerous molecules. In the typical marine aquarium, ionic calcium has two main fates: uptake by inhabitants for biological utilization or becoming bound with free carbonate ions and other divalent cations to form highly insoluble carbonate salts. Of these, calcium carbonate ($CaCO_3$) is of most interest to aquarium hobbyists.

Calcium Carbonate

There are two crystalline forms of $CaCO_3$: calcite and aragonite. Calcite, which is the predominant constituent of materials such as limestone and marble, is much less soluble than aragonite, and is therefore of limited use in a marine aquarium. By contrast, aragonite dissociates readily in the presence of a weak acid, thereby releasing the carbonate to buffer pH and the calcium to be incorporated into the tissues and skeletal components of aquatic organisms. The greater solubility of aragonite in seawater accounts for its widespread use throughout the marine aquarium hobby both as a substrate and as a medium in calcium reactors. The formation/dissolution reaction of calcium carbonate is presented in Eq. 8.1.

(Eq. 8.1)

$$CaCO_{3(s)} \leftrightarrow Ca^{2+}_{(aq)} + CO_3^{2-}{}_{(aq)}$$

In the presence of an acid, the carbonate (CO_3^{2-}) and bicarbonate (HCO_3^-) act as proton acceptors, via Eqs. 8.2 and 8.3. In doing so, they help prevent pH from lowering.

(Eq. 8.2)

$$H^+_{(aq)} + CO_3^{2-}{}_{(aq)} \leftrightarrow HCO_3^-{}_{(aq)}$$

(Eq. 8.3)

$$HCO_3^-{}_{(aq)} + H^+_{(aq)} \leftrightarrow H_2CO_{3(aq)}$$

As demonstrated, carbonic acid (H_2CO_3) is the end result. In turn, the carbonic acid exists in equilibrium with carbon dioxide and water, shown in Eq. 8.4.

(Eq. 8.4)

$$CO_{2(g)} + H_2O_{(l)} \leftrightarrow H_2CO_{3(aq)}$$

This equation also illustrates that carbon dioxide dissolved in water will form a weak acid that causes pH to decrease. At night, when photosynthetic organisms stop photosynthesizing but continue to respire oxygen and produce carbon dioxide, the pH in an aquarium typically drops. Without adequate alkalinity in the system, this nightly drop in pH would become greater with passing time, eventually causing distress to the livestock.

Calcium carbonate is one of the major building blocks for the tests, shells, skeletons, and tubes of many plankton, mollusks, corals, bony fishes, certain algae, and polychaete worms, respectively. Without a sufficient concentration of calcium and carbonates in the system, these organisms cannot be expected to grow at normal rates, regardless of other parameters. While different types of organisms have their own requirements for these ions in seawater, the hobbyist's ultimate goal generally should be to provide calcium and carbonates in concentrations needed by the most $CaCO_3$-demanding organism in the system, and this is fundamentally accomplished by maintaining natural seawater concentrations of both ions at all times. If the calcium concentration in the aquarium falls below the natural seawater concentration, the rate at which new

▲ *Corals and other marine invertebrates that secrete aragonite to form their skeletal structure, like this branching* Montipora sp.*, will not show appreciable growth unless the concentrations of calcium, magnesium, strontium, and carbonates fall within the recommended ranges.*

calcareous skeletal and shell material forms is greatly depressed.

In general, the goal in reef systems is to maintain the calcium concentration between 412 and 450 mg/L, accomplished by using calcium additives and/or a calcium reactor, both of which may be aided by a bed of aragonite in the system. Note that maintaining the recommended concentration of calcium is much more important in reef systems than in those housing only fishes, in which regular water changes with a quality salt mix will provide enough calcium to satisfy the needs of the inhabitants.

Calcium Reactors

Calcium reactors are semi-enclosed vessels that provide calcium ions via the dissolution of calcareous media or some calcium-bearing salt. Such systems have come quite a long way in the past few years, and have subsequently gained a strong following among advanced reef hobbyists. There are two main variations on calcium reaction systems: those that use aragonite media and those that use kalkwasser $Ca(OH)_2$ solution (widely known as Nilsen reactors, after their inventor, long-time hobbyist Alf Nilsen). One aspect these units share is their high price tags, but they can sometimes be worth every penny, particularly on large aquarium systems with high stocking densities of reef-building organisms.

▲ ***The suggested levels of calcium, magnesium, strontium, and carbonates for a marine tank closely mirror natural seawater concentrations. These chemical requirements must be met regardless of the lighting and filtration systems utilized if corals and various other organisms are to thrive in captivity.***

Traditional calcium reactors filter aquarium water injected with CO_2 gas through a bed of aragonite. The slightly depressed pH of the water within the reaction vessel causes the aragonite to dissolve at a relatively high rate, supplying the aquarium with calcium, carbonate, and many ancillary constituents of the material, such as magnesium, strontium, and a small host of trace elements. To control the rate of aragonite dissolution, the rate of CO_2 must be carefully regulated with an electronic pH controller. Excess CO_2 from calcium reactors have been implicated in problems with microalgal proliferation throughout the display aquarium in several instances, so using a pH controller with one of these units is not so much an option as it is a necessity. Once a calcium reactor system has been set up to maintain the calcium and carbonate levels in the aquarium, very little additional tinkering is needed. Given time to make minor adjustments and fine-tune their operation, calcium reactors truly are a great innovation and tool in the reef aquarium hobby.

The hurdle that many reef hobbyists simply can't overcome is the price of putting together a calcium reactor system, regardless of whether certain components are homemade; some of the premium models and systems command prices in the $500 to $800 range. This includes the reaction column or vessel, a pressurized CO_2 canister and regulator valve, electronic pH controller, electronic or magnetic solenoid valve, and reaction media. Fortunately, more-affordable systems are entering the market and will make this approach available to a larger number of hobbyists.

Controlling pH with Sulfur

A newer method[1] of aragonite dissolution is to use sulfate to depress pH within the reaction vessel. This method is actually a spin-off of a sulfur-fed denitrification filter system, in which a sulfurous medium is placed within a semi-enclosed vessel and utilized as a growth and colonization medium for the bacteria responsible for nitrate reduction. When the flow rate of water through the medium is properly adjusted, the result is a total reduction in nitrate (into nitrogen gas) and the release of sulfate. If this sulfate-laden (hence low-pH) water is then passed through a column of calcareous media, the result is dissolution of the media, producing the same results obtained with a traditional calcium reactor but at a fraction the cost, with no associated CO_2-related issues, and with the total eradication

[1] While this method is new to many aquarium hobbyists, it has been in use for well over a decade in large-scale aquaria and scientific institutions throughout parts of Europe.

Large-polyp stony corals are as dependent upon available calcium as their small-polyp stony relatives are. This is a beautiful specimen that was damaged during transport, yet which recovered and is growing rapidly as a result of having its chemical and lighting requirements met.

of nitrate. This system represents the current cutting edge of reef aquarium water care technology.

Nilsen Reactors

Nilsen reactors can be thought of, in a nutshell, as a less expensive means of automated calcium addition than traditional calcium reactors. A complete Nilsen reactor system can be assembled from scratch for upwards of $250, depending on the quality of materials used; additionally, several manufacturers offer units for sale at reasonable prices. There are numerous designs, all pioneered by do-it-yourself reef hobbyists, but the basic premise is a reaction chamber sealed from the atmosphere in which a saturated kalkwasser solution is locally circulated (either periodically or continuously), and into which purified water is pumped (again, either periodically or continuously) in order to force kalkwasser solution into the aquarium. Kalkwasser and its use are discussed in more detail shortly, but for now it may be stated that the end result is increased calcium concentration and higher pH of the solution, and hence the aquarium system as a whole.

Just as with traditional calcium reactors, Nilsen reactors are best used in conjunction with a pH controller, though in this instance the goal is to prevent pH of the aquarium itself from rising *too high*. The setup is as follows: a reaction chamber (preferably clear, such as an acrylic tube) is filled with purified water and kalkwasser (amount used contingent upon overall volume of the chamber). The solution must be occasionally stirred, either by a submersible pump, mechanical stirring rod, or magnetic stirring platform, stirring bar, or cross; this keeps the material at the bottom of the chamber slightly fluid. The chamber is sealed, with one port in, through which fresh purified water will enter the chamber, and one port out, through which kalkwasser solution will enter the aquarium.

The ideal setup is to have water enter the reaction chamber only when the pH of the aquarium water drops below a certain point; this is accomplished by plugging the pump in the freshwater reservoir into a pH controller, the probe of which is located somewhere in the aquarium system. In this fashion, water only enters (and kalkwasser solution exits) the chamber when needed. Some hobbyists prefer the system to be in continuous, rather than sporadic, operation to maximize the amount of calcium entering the system per unit time. Unfortunately, many hobbyists discover that this maximum rate of calcium addition can't keep the residual calcium concentration in their reef aquaria above the natural seawater concentration. This is at least partly due to the fact that the high pH of kalkwasser solution limits

▲ *Hippopus hippopus*, *sometimes called the "horse-hoof" clam, grows relatively slowly compared to its relatives in the genus* Tridacna, *but all members of this family share the same requirements for adequate available calcium, requiring monitored calcium supplementation as needed.*

the maximum rate at which the solution may be added to the aquarium, hence limiting calcium supplementation.

Aragonite Sand

Placing a layer of aragonite sand on the bottom of the aquarium has been gaining popularity in the hobby over the past few years. Benefits of having such a substrate in an aquarium include a more natural appearance (as compared to leaving the bottom of the aquarium bare); gradual release of minute amounts of calcium, carbonate, magnesium, strontium, and trace elements into the system; larger capacity for bacterial colonization and hence biological filtration by simple virtue of the added surface area; and providing a substrate for burrowing and sand-sifting livestock to set up residence and search for food. The gradual dissolution of aragonite has gained a reputation for being able to buffer water and release calcium to such magnitude that supplemental addition of buffering and calcium products is not required.

While this may be true in systems with a low to modest requirement for buffering and calcium, it is unlikely that these circumstances are common in most well-stocked reef aquarium systems. Under "normal" conditions, the rate of calcium and carbonate uptake by reef-building organisms is simply greater than the rate at which aragonite will naturally dissolve to release these components. One way to try and cheat the system is to use a relatively deep bed of aragonite sand on the bottom of the aquarium or in a refugium underlaid with sulfurous media as described previously in sulfate-based calcium and nitrate reaction, and hope that the release of sulfate and other weak acids by bacteria living on and within the substrate is sufficient to cause the aragonite to dissolve at an accelerated rate.

Calcium Supplementation

The degree to which a calcium reactor will work is largely dictated by the aquarium's specific chemical and biological details and the nature of the calcium-bearing media employed. Somewhat ironically, it often becomes necessary to supplement a reef aquarium with additional calcium to maintain the concentration within the desired range. This is often the exception rather than the rule, and hobbyists having good results with these reactors swear by them.

Calcium Additives

Calcium additives are considered by many to be the method of choice for keeping the calcium concentration in reef aquaria within the desired range. They are easy to use, economical, and produce the desired results when used in conjunction with accurate test kits. On the other hand, there are those reef hobbyists that shun all additives, regardless of chemical nature. It's very important to state that *not all additives and supplements are created equal.* Something to keep in mind is that niche products such as aquarium supplements are best purchased from a manufacturer that deals *mainly* in that area of the market; this is largely due to quality control, or in the case of mass-market manufacturers, lack thereof.

Solid vs. Liquid

Products that increase the calcium concentration are available in both solid (powder, pelletized, or granular) and liquid forms. In general, liquid products offer the simplest form of supplementation: shake the bottle for a few seconds, pop the lid, and add the volume required for your system as directed by the indications on the label. This is in direct opposition of dry products, which generally require that the supplement be measured out carefully, mixed into solution in a separate container, and dosed either gradually or all at once. The

Popular some years ago, bare-bottom setups like this one are giving way to ones with an aragonite substrate, both to increase biofiltration and to provide a boost to important mineral concentrations from the slowly dissolving aragonite.

advantage of using dry products is that they're much more cost effective than prepared solutions, providing more bang for the buck (for an extensive discussion of this topic, please refer to Appendix V). Among the most commonly encountered calcium supplements are calcium hydroxide (also known by the German name for "chalk water," kalkwasser), calcium chloride, calcium gluconate, calcium EDTA, and calcium carbonate.

Solutions

When discussing water care supplements and the manner in which they impact the chemistry of aquarium water, it is important to understand the basic principles of solutions as chemically defined. A **solution** can be described for our purposes as a condition in which some solute such as a salt (an ionic solid composed of cations and anions other than H^+ and OH^-) is dissolved in water. When a salt is completely dissolved in water, the end result is cations and anions tumbling around and only briefly interacting with each other as they come into close proximity with ions of the opposite charge. If the temperature and atmospheric pressure of the solution

◀ ***Giant clams of the genus Tridacna. Long-term success with this group of invertebrates often seems to be hit-or-miss. It is possible that a dietary deficiency is responsible for the decline and/or demise of specimens that have appeared to be perfectly healthy and then perished, in spite of no outward changes in water chemistry, lighting, or behavior of tank-mates.***

remain constant and no other substances are added, the solution would remain unchanged forever (in theory). If calcium chloride is used as an example, the calcium and chloride ions would remain in a perpetual aqueous state (dissolved in the water) rather than recombining to precipitate out of solution. Even if other water soluble salts were added to the solution, so long as the solution remains below the solubility equilibrium it is unlikely that any long-term interactions will occur, so again it can be stated that all ions will remain in solution (i.e. dissolved).

If, on the other hand, some substance that had a high affinity for attracting ions of the opposite charge, such as carbonate or phosphate anions, were added to the solution, reactions would take place between these anions and any cations present in the solution—in this case, calcium. The end result would be the formation of insoluble precipitants, and the extent to which precipitants were formed, as well as the composition of those precipitants, would depend on the initial concentrations of the ions involved and their affinities for bonding with each other. This scenario can be broadened to consider the aquarium water itself as a solution containing a plethora of ions, as well as other substances such as organic molecules and gases. Considering the total number, as well as the individual concentrations, of substances present in seawater, the grounds are set for a multiplicity of reactions to take place when conditions are conducive; knowing which reactions are probable can help a hobbyist make better decisions about which

Calcium Hydroxide ($Ca(OH)_2$)	
Pros	Cons
51% calcium by dry weight	Can cause the pH of the aquarium water to rise dangerously
Can help maintain pH in aquarium if dosing of the solution is controlled properly	May not be able to satisfy the calcium demand of the aquarium
Will not alter the ionic ratio of seawater	May contain trace amounts of silicate
	Lengthy preparation process

supplements to purchase, and how to use them to best advantage.

Kalkwasser

Calcium hydroxide ($Ca(OH)_2$), or **kalkwasser**, is perhaps the most familiar powdered calcium supplement available to marine aquarium hobbyists. By dry weight, calcium hydroxide is over 51% calcium, which is a greater percentage than can be found among the other calcium supplements available to reef hobbyists. The drawback, as briefly alluded to in the discussion of Nilsen reactors, is that saturated kalkwasser solution has a high pH (approximately 12.00 to 12.50), owing to the concentration of hydroxide ions released during dissociation; this places limits on the rate at which kalkwasser solution can safely be added to the system, and hence limits the rate at which calcium is added. Additionally, calcium hydroxide has relatively low solubility in water: one gram in half a U.S. gallon (64 ounces) of purified water is near saturation.

The steps involved with preparing and dosing kalkwasser solution are as follows: in a clean container, mix up to two teaspoons of calcium hydroxide in each gallon of purified water, cover the container, gently mix the water, and allow the solution to stand for at least two hours to allow any undissolved calcium hydroxide to settle to the bottom of the container; draw the kalkwasser solution from above this layer of sediment, and drip it slowly into the system. As noted, the rate at which the solution can be dripped will depend on the extent to which it affects the pH of the system. Dripping it too quickly can cause the pH to rise outside the recommended range. For this reason, many hobbyists prefer to drip kalkwasser solution at night, when the pH of the aquarium system tends to be at its lowest due to a net increase in carbonic acid during that period.

Owing to the restraints placed on the rate of kalkwasser solution addition to a system, it becomes clear why this practice is often unable to raise and maintain calcium concentrations in a

▲ *Since large doses can cause dangerous spikes in pH, kalwasser drip is best added to an aquarium at night, when pH is typically lowest due to a lack of photosynthetic activity.*

reef aquarium without additional supplementation from another calcium source. To illustrate, consider a reef aquarium in which the average daily drop in the calcium concentration is 10 mg/L (due to uptake by the various inhabitants as well as precipitation and temporary bonds with various ions and molecules). If the maximum allowable rate of kalkwasser solution addition to the system doesn't supply that 10 mg/L over a 24-hour period, the calcium concentration in the system will begin to drop. This is a common enough problem, and one that is most easily solved by using another source of calcium that doesn't have a direct effect on pH (or alkalinity, if possible) in addition to the kalkwasser solution, or as a complete alternative. Granted, this is not always the case; experimentation in each system is required to determine whether or not kalkwasser alone will be capable of maintaining the desired calcium concentration.

One other aspect of kalkwasser is that it tends to contain a small percentage of silicate. The extent to which the silicate contributed can cause diatom growth in a reef aquarium is on a case-by-case basis, and most hobbyists using kalkwasser to the maximum capability will never observe negative effects from the miniscule amount of silicate that is inadvertently added.

One of the benefits of using kalkwasser is that it can help decrease the phosphate concentration in a system by forming calcium-phosphate compounds of low solubility.

(Eq. 8.5)

$$3\ Ca^{2+} + 2\ PO_4^{3-} \leftrightarrow Ca_3(PO_4)_2$$

This reaction is similar to that between calcium ions and carbonate ions, except that in this case the anion is a phosphate compound. Continuous use of kalkwasser, or any other source of inorganic calcium, depletes phosphate with time, though this method should not be relied upon as a means of primary phosphate removal; doing so would not only waste a good deal of calcium but also indicates that the aquarium is not balanced with respect to nutrient addition and removal. Be advised that high phosphate concentrations in an aquarium can deplete the calcium concentration by the same method as that outlined above, so if difficulty increasing and maintaining the calcium concentration in a reef aquarium is observed, testing the phosphate concentration is warranted. It's important to state that *any* free calcium ions, regardless of their original source, can and will interact with phosphate ions in this manner. An excessively high concentration of phosphate can negatively affect the calcium concentration in a reef aquarium, a subject discussed at greater length in the chapter dealing with phosphate and organic matter.

One great aspect about kalkwasser is that it does not alter the ionic ratio of the aquarium water, because it's composed of nothing more than calcium and hydroxide. In the minds of advanced reef hobbyists, this fact alone gives kalkwasser an advantage over other calcium salts.

Calcium Chloride

Calcium chloride (CaCl2) is a calcium supplement that most reef hobbyists will turn to at one time or another. Not quite as strong as kalkwasser in terms of total calcium percentage by weight, calcium chloride has a strong following due to the fact that a solution is simple to prepare and subsequently administer to an aquarium; calcium chloride can be mixed with a cup of purified water and added directly to the aquarium all at once with little to no obvious effect on pH. Because it boasts this advantage of having relaxed constraints on dosing rate, a calcium chloride solution rarely has any difficulty with increasing and maintaining the calcium

▲ ***A substrate that includes aragonite sand offers sand-sifting grazers like this yellow sea cucumber a good place to live and eat.***

Calcium Chloride ($CaCl_2$)	
Pros	Cons
Up to 35% calcium by dry weight	Can alter ionic ratio of seawater with continued use and infrequent water changes
Will not directly affect pH of aquarium water	Can cause alkalinity to drop if dosed too rapidly
Simple preparation process	

▲ ***Low magnesium concentrations can adversely affect the levels of calcium in an aquarium, so a dearth of the former should be the first suspect if maintaining the latter becomes difficult.***

concentration in even the most heavily stocked reef aquarium to within the desired range, all other things being equal.

One potential problem associated with this ability to deluge the aquarium with calcium ions is that alkalinity may decrease as a result, due to interaction between calcium ions and the bicarbonate ions largely responsible for buffering the system. So long as the dose of calcium to the system isn't too heavy, this scenario can generally be avoided; simply don't saturate the system with calcium ions (this applies to any calcium supplement, though it's more commonplace when using calcium chloride solutions). Hobbyists previously unfamiliar with this side effect of calcium chloride often find out the hard way. In most cases, they observe a slight drop in alkalinity when they exceed the maximum allowable calcium concentration in the aquarium and/or the aqueous magnesium concentration in the aquarium is inadequate. If the alkalinity drops below the level to which acids present in the water can be neutralized, the pH will begin to drop. This is a scenario that can be avoided by following the manufacturer's directions and paying attention to water parameters.

(Eq. 8.6)

$$CaCl_{2(aq)} \leftrightarrow Ca^{2+}{}_{(aq)} + 2Cl^{-}{}_{(aq)}$$

(Eq. 8.7)

$$Ca^{2+}{}_{(aq)} + CO_3{}^{2-}{}_{(aq)} \leftrightarrow CaCO_{3(s)}$$

Chloride Imbalance

Most advanced hobbyists would deem a discussion of calcium chloride without mention of "chloride imbalance" to be incomplete. If during the course of maintaining the concentration of some parameter, one were to add copious amounts of a conservative substance, the concentration of that substance would continue to increase with each addition. Many hobbyists fear such a scenario, particularly when it comes to adding calcium chloride to a reef aquarium. While calcium is utilized by various life forms in the system, it is

◀ ***While so-called "chloride imbalances" are plausible, it is not at all clear what their potential damage to the denizens of reef aquaria is.***

reasoned that chloride ions, with no major mechanism for removal, keep increasing in concentration, which ultimately can cause aquarium inhabitants to die. In this manner, the ionic ratio of the seawater (the ratio of abundance of each ion species relative to the other ions in the water) is said to be in an imbalance. While the concept is plausible, its proposed impact on aquarium inhabitants is largely exaggerated. Consider the following:

- The composition of salt blends will differ from manufacturer to manufacturer; already, the ionic ratio of the water is imbalanced compared to natural seawater.

- Chloride is the most abundant ion in natural seawater, at a mean concentration of 19,500 mg/L, and the fact that during normal dosing not much chloride is entering the system relative to that already existing there.

- It is practically impossible to legitimately diagnose a problem as

Organic Calcium

Something that should sound an alarm in the reader's head is the fact that such a small percentage of the organic calcium molecule is actually calcium. Even in the best-case scenario, in which the molecule is 12% calcium by dry weight, the remaining 88% of the molecule is organic material. Imagine trying to maintain the calcium concentration in a heavily stocked reef aquarium (which has a high calcium demand) with a product that admits over seven times as much organic material as it does calcium, and one begins to see the inherent problem with this approach. This method is also more costly to the user, as it may take twice as much of an organic calcium product to achieve the same calcium concentration obtained by many calcium chloride solutions available, and organic calcium supplements are typically more expensive than alternate calcium sources.

being due to chloride imbalance. What *exactly* are the symptoms?

- At least 10% of the total water volume in the aquarium is supposed to be changed and replaced with freshly made seawater once weekly, which would help serve to dilute the increasing chloride concentration.

Don't worry about chloride imbalance. Simply follow the directions on the label of your calcium chloride solution, perform regular water changes, and monitor the water quality and appearance of the aquarium residents. These should all be normal tasks for aquarium hobbyists. Calcium chloride can be a very valuable supplement to quickly raise and maintain the calcium concentration in an aquarium system.

Calcium Gluconate and Calcium EDTA	
Pros	Cons
Will not directly affect pH of aquarium water	Only 9 to 12% calcium by dry weight in most cases
Will not interact with other ions in solution	Can overload an aquarium with organic material
	Must generally be refrigerated or preserved in solution
	Organic calcium may have limited effectiveness

Organic Calcium

Calcium gluconate and **calcium EDTA** are often termed "organic calcium," as the molecules to which the calcium ions are bound are organic, rather than inorganic, in nature. There is a fair amount of complexity that accompanies a discussion of these supplements, one that could range all over this book; reading further will familiarize hobbyists with the reasons that additions of organic matter to a marine aquarium are best limited.

The basic idea behind the use of organic calcium was that it would be easily taken up by reef-building organisms such as corals and clams, and in doing so would increase the rate of growth of these organisms. Organic molecules, it has been found, are rapidly absorbed into living cell tissue; therefore, using them as

▲ *Provided with adequate calcium levels, this colony grew from a small cluster of branches, and over the course of a year doubled in size. It is difficult, however, to maintain water quality when organic sources of calcium are the sole additive.*

transport mechanisms to deliver calcium directly to the organisms that needed it seemed to be logical. An additional benefit of the stability of organic calcium is that it doesn't interact with other ions in solution until the bond between the organic molecule and the calcium ion are broken; this means that the calcium is considered more bioavailable, to an extent, because it won't bond with anions such as carbonate or phosphate and fall out of solution. With regular use, dosing one of these organic calcium supplements in a reef can have impressive results for the first few weeks–corals and clams appear to inflate more fully and even seem to grow at a more rapid pace than when inorganic calcium sources alone are utilized.

When using these products as the sole source of calcium in a reef aquarium, however, signs of an organic overload often begin to appear unless large, frequent water changes are made. Over the course of a few days, the animals that had once looked so full begin to deflate, and this is often accompanied by faint cloudiness of the aquarium water. Like a child fed a continuous diet of candy, the aquarium residents initially appear full of life and vigor, but as time goes on, their systems can no longer cope with the hyperactive metabolism fueled by the sugar, and they appear to go into a state of shock. The reef inhabitants aren't the only organisms that temporarily benefit from the increased concentration of organic matter in the system. Bacteria also take advantage of this food source, and in doing so, reproduce to a population density that will only peak once the abundance of food begins to decline, evident when the aquarium begins to cloud; this cloud is a massive die-off of bacteria that have largely depleted their food source. This isn't to say that all the food is gone, merely that the food that's available can't support such a dense population of bacteria. As the bacteria die and begin to decompose, pH and the dissolved oxygen concentration in the system begin to decline, and if allowed to proceed too far will begin to negatively impact the rest of the aquarium inhabitants. This is a costly mistake, though not all systems will have this problem (systems with very efficient protein skimmers *sometimes* get by without incident). There are many variables to consider, such as the amount of the product being used on a daily basis per unit volume of water in the aquarium, the types and stocking density of organisms in the aquarium, water temperature, and overall efficiency of filtration, to name a few. All of these aspects will influence the overall effect organic calcium can have on an aquarium. The use of a redox, or ORP, meter would help avoid this entire scenario, as the gradually decreasing ORP of the water would indicate that the concentration of organic material in the system was approaching an unsafe level, signaling that it was time to stop using the product and/or perform a very large water change.

A beautiful stony coral, captive raised from a fragment, for sale at an aquarium retail shop. Although it may take several months for a fragment to grow into such a large colony, many hobbyists feel that the reward is worth the wait. This type of growth cannot occur unless dissolved mineral concentrations are kept up and dissolved organic concentrations are kept down.

Organic calcium products are available as solutions, and bacteria entering the solution at any point during the manufacturing process will feast on the organic material unless they are somehow prohibited, either chemically or by lowering the temperature in the solution to the point at which bacterial activity slows to a crawl, or ceases completely. Therefore, such product must be preserved by the manufacturer and/or refrigerated after opening, to prevent spoiling. This isn't necessarily grounds for avoiding the product, unless the manufacturer uses bactericidal preservatives, which can kill not only the bacteria in the product but also those responsible for maintaining the nitrogen cycle in the aquarium itself.

Bottles of chelated calcium solutions that appear to have black material around the mouth or floating throughout the solution are showing signs of bacterial proliferation and should be discarded completely or returned to the manufacturer for a refund.

While organic calcium can certainly have some benefits to the reef aquarium, there are many negative attributes that come into play under "use as directed," too many for products that contain a mere 9 to 12% calcium by dry weight, and even less in solution.

Calcium Carbonate

Although calcium carbonate ($CaCO_3$) is only slightly soluble in water, there are ways that a powdered aragonite supplement can benefit a reef system in the same manner as a calcium reactor, and with much less expense. The trade-off is the amount of time involved in doing so effectively, or more specifically, in order for the aragonite to benefit a reef aquarium in the same magnitude as other calcium supplements. There is a quandary involved with adding calcium carbonate to the system: once the point of saturation is reached, no more calcium carbonate will dissolve; however, if the system is *gradually* dosed with calcium carbonate, rather than adding a copious amount of it at one time, the water is less likely to reach this saturation point (or at the very least it will take longer to reach it), and the powder will continue to dissolve into solution. Hence, this method affords the same benefits of a calcium reactor, but in a more high-maintenance manner. One way to potentially bypass this limitation is to utilize powdered aragonite in a Nilsen reactor; this automated approach

Calcium Carbonate ($CaCO_3$)	
Pros	**Cons**
39% calcium by dry weight	Low solubility in water limits effectiveness
Will not directly affect pH of aquarium water	Must be added several times daily in small doses to obtain desired results
Simple preparation process	
Increases concentrations of calcium and carbonate ions in aquarium	

▲ *While zoanthids and similar colonial polyps do not deplete calcium as rapidly as their stony coral relatives, the element is nonetheless important to their growth and long-term survival.*

eliminates the high-pH issue involved with the use of kalkwasser, though the constraint on calcium carbonate saturation in the system still exists. While the rate of dosing this calcium carbonate-rich solution may be faster than can be safely accomplished when using kalkwasser solution, the question is whether or not this accelerated dosing rate can make up for the difference in calcium percentage (calcium carbonate contains less calcium by dry weight than calcium hydroxide); this will depend largely on the ease with

Supplement Ingredients

A point worth briefly discussing is that unlike products meant for human consumption, there are no federal rules governing the order in which ingredients are listed in aquarium water care supplements. In other words, simply because the manufacturer states on the label that the first ingredient (which on most other labels means it's the most abundant) in a solution is calcium, this is not necessarily true. In fact in this case, it's impossible. On occasion, one might see a liquid product in which calcium is listed as a main ingredient (before water), yet when poured into a clear container, the product appears clear, colorless, and contains no sediment. A product in which a calcium salt, or any other ionic solid, was in more abundance than water would be very thick, almost like a cake, so it's apparent that the label is misrepresenting the relative amounts of the product's contents.

which pH is influenced in each individual aquarium system.

Testing the calcium concentration in the reef aquarium should be done on a weekly basis, regardless of the apparent stability of the water chemistry. As a reef hobbyist becomes more knowledgeable and familiar with the appearance of healthy organisms in the aquarium, he or she will be more able to detect when the water quality is acceptable and when it's lacking in some aspect. However, without formal testing of the water, there's often no way to say with certainty exactly *what* parameter needs to be re-adjusted. Quality test kits should not be considered an *option* for aquarium hobbyists; they are insurance with which the considerable investment in animal life, time, and money can be protected from unnecessary losses. Please refer to the section discussing test kit selection for aspects to consider prior to purchasing new test kits.

CHAPTER 9

Strontium

Though **strontium** is a widely used supplement in the marine aquarium hobby, its role in ocean water is not well documented in marine aquarium literature. Strontium is an element similar to calcium; it's taken up rapidly by corals, mollusks, and tubeworms, and incorporated into their skeletons as strontium carbonate ($SrCO_3$) and other molecules, much the same way calcium is. The average strontium concentration in ocean water is approximately 8 mg/L, though observations of many seasoned hobbyists indicate that maintaining a concentration of 10 to 15 mg/L seems to increase the growth rate of corals and giant clams. Just as with calcium, strontium supplements are available in dry and liquid form.

Strontium Chloride ($SrCl_2$)	
Pros	Cons
32% strontium by dry weight, on average	Can alter ionic ratio of seawater with continued use and infrequent water changes
Will not directly affect pH of aquarium water	Can cause alkalinity to decrease if dosed too rapidly
Simple preparation process	

The presence of an adequate concentration of strontium in a reef aquarium has been implicated in the ability to help prevent coral tissue from peeling away from the skeleton; at the same time, it has been described as a toxin. Strontium, as strontium carbonate ($SrCO_3$) is generally found in the same deposits

as calcium carbonate, such as in shells, coral skeletons, and other aragonite parts secreted by invertebrates, which would seem to indicate that at the very least it's taken up by reef-building organisms; in fact, it's thought that strontium helps form the seed crystal that encourages accumulation of calcium in predominantly calcium carbonate minerals. Therefore, at natural seawater concentrations, claims about toxicity of strontium to marine organisms would seem to be rather implausible. Even maintained at higher concentrations than those found in natural seawater, strontium does not outwardly appear to negatively affect reef aquarium inhabitants, so perhaps the bottom line is that even though the precise roles that strontium plays for reef inhabitants are not crystal clear, logic would seem to indicate that these

◀ *A Picture is Worth 1,000 Words* ▲
Before and after photos of a brain coral, Trachyphyllia sp. ***The first photo is of the specimen maintained in a system in which strontium was not supplemented, while the second photo shows the same specimen after six months in a system that received regular addition of a strontium salt to maintain the natural seawater strontium concentration. All other parameters, including lighting, remained the same. This may not offer any conclusive evidence that strontium benefits corals and other marine organisms, but it certainly appears to.***

organisms are better off with it than without.

Strontium chloride ($SrCl_2$) is the most common ingredient of strontium supplements available to aquarium hobbyists. Because strontium is present in ocean water in a relatively small concentration, it takes very little strontium chloride to maintain the desired concentration in a reef aquarium. Most solutions of strontium chloride are therefore quite dilute, and powdered strontium chloride supplements will last most reef hobbyists several months, if not years. Because such a small amount of strontium chloride need be added to a reef aquarium, the chance for alkalinity depletion when the product is used as directed is essentially nonexistent.

(Eq. 9.1)

$$SrCl_{2(aq)} \leftrightarrow Sr2^{+}{}_{(aq)} + 2Cl^{-}{}_{(aq)}$$

(Eq. 9.2)

$$Sr^{2+}{}_{(aq)} + CO_3{}^{2-}{}_{(aq)} \leftrightarrow SrCO_{3(s)}$$

Unfortunately, and owing to the apparent difficulty with which strontium is isolated, there do not appear to be any strontium test kits for aquarium use that are cost effective and/or very accurate, which leaves determination of the strontium concentration in an aquarium largely to estimation based on the overall volume of the system and the means by which strontium is dosed. A strontium supplement should list the percentage of strontium present, and from that and the rate of dosing a hobbyist will be able to perform some simple calculations to get a sensible idea of the overall strontium concentration in the aquarium (see Appendix V).

Alternately, the problem can be approached from the opposite angle: use the concentration of strontium in the product to determine the weight or volume required to achieve the desired concentration in the aquarium prior to dosing it. This method is somewhat complicated by the presence of strontium in synthetic sea salt, but it's better than nothing, and probably accurate enough to enable the maintenance of a strontium concentration within a range of 8 to 15 mg/L. Many hobbyists find that they can provide the necessary strontium to their reef aquaria by using a premium salt blend and performing regular water changes.

CHAPTER 10

Magnesium

Because very little has been written about magnesium in aquarium literature, the important role it plays in seawater has not been sufficiently emphasized to reef aquarium hobbyists, many of which would likely find calcium supplementation more manageable when armed with this information.

Magnesium is present in seawater at an average concentration of 1,288 mg/L. It serves an important purpose by preventing free calcium ions from immediately bonding with free carbonates. As outlined in the following paragraph, this is accomplished by the formation of ion pairs between carbonate and magnesium ions (Mg^{2+}), leaving calcium ions available for uptake by reef-building corals and other invertebrates. In turn, the bonds between the magnesium and carbonate are broken easily enough to allow the carbonate to buffer pH depressions and be used by the inhabitants as needed.

Weak interactions between ions are constantly taking place as they move past one another in water. The greater the overall concentration of ions in the solution, the greater the frequency of these interactions, and the more significant they become in determining the availability of substances for biological and chemical reactions to occur. Interactions between ions of opposite charge ultimately lead to the

▲ ***Don't overlook two of the biggest sinks of calcium, magnesium, strontium, and carbonates in reef aquaria: calcareous algae such as*** **Halimeda** ***sp. and coralline algae. The rapid growth of these organisms under optimal conditions is a result of their ability to extract the components of aragonite from the surrounding water.***

formation of ion pairs (having ionic bonds) or complexes (having covalent bonds). Ion pairs are typically formed between a pair of polyvalent ions or one polyvalent and one monovalent ion. It is the former case that applies to magnesium, calcium, and carbonate ions. Approximately 67% of the carbonate ions in seawater exist in ion pairs with magnesium, as compared to only 7% of the total carbonate paired with calcium; the vast difference in the concentration of magnesium to that of calcium (1,290 ppm vs. 412 ppm) illustrates the point that $MgCO_3$ forms far more readily in seawater than $CaCO_3$.

(Eq. 10.1)

$$\mathbf{Mg^{2+}_{(aq)} + CO_3^{2-}_{(aq)} \leftrightarrow MgCO_{3(s)}}$$

In a reef aquarium, the magnesium concentration should be maintained within a range of 1,290 to 1,320 mg/L. Because of the expense of quality magnesium salts, synthetic sea salt blends often lack adequate magnesium; blends formulated for fish-only aquaria may have less than half the magnesium concentration recommended for reef aquaria[1]. In such cases it becomes necessary to resort to magnesium supplementation, or simply to switch to a brand of salt that contains the magnesium concentration of natural seawater. Ultimately, keeping the magnesium concentration within the recommended range will simplify maintenance of alkalinity and calcium levels.

Magnesium is also used during the production of chlorophyll, and activates some of the enzymes utilized by photosynthetic organisms, such as the symbiotic zooxanthellae living within the tissues of hermatypic organisms, as well as by macroalgae. Inadequate magnesium in a reef aquarium can therefore have a direct impact on corals, giant clams, and their respective allies.

Test Kits

Magnesium test kits for marine aquaria are available from many manufacturers. Performing a magnesium test on a new brand of salt when making a change from one product to another will indicate the amount of magnesium supplementation that may be required to maintain the natural seawater concentration; this step is strongly recommended for reef aquarium hobbyists, particularly those maintaining aquaria heavily stocked with reef-building organisms. As part of general aquarium maintenance, testing the magnesium concentration should be performed at least once each month. If maintaining the calcium concentration in a reef aquarium becomes excessively difficult for no apparent reason, it's likely that insufficient magnesium is the culprit and this is easily remedied.

[1] Nearly half of the cost of raw materials used in premium salt blends may be components of magnesium. This is one of the aspects that separate premium salt blends from inexpensive, low-end blends.

CHAPTER 11

Iodine

Although it has long been known that **iodine** is important in marine aquaria, particularly reef systems, there is little credible information offered to aquarists as to why this is so. In order to discuss this topic, it is prudent to make the distinction between iodine and iodide, and briefly review the role each plays in a system with living organisms.

The sum of concentrations of iodine species, principally iodide (I^-) and iodate (IO_3^-), in natural seawater is approximately 0.06 mg/L. Iodine behaves non-conservatively in an aquarium; livestock depletes it and chemical filtration and protein skimming remove it from the system, requiring regular iodine supplementation to maintain a measurable concentration and provide benefits to inhabitants.

Iodine may very well be one of the most important elements present in a reef aquarium; its concentration is usually a limiting factor in the rate of metabolism and growth of fishes and invertebrates. Without a sufficient concentration of iodine in the water, fishes will often develop goiter, crustaceans will not molt, certain types of macroalgae will not survive, soft corals will gradually die, corals in general will show poorly (iodide affects pigmentation), *Xenia* and *Anthelia* won't thrive and may die back, and the list continues. Iodide may be very important to hermatypic invertebrates as a means to help detoxify excess oxygen produced by their symbiotic zooxanthellae under supraoptimal light. See the following equations for a possible mechanism:

(Eq. 11.1)

$$6\ CO_2 + 6\ H_2O \xrightarrow{\text{light energy}} C_6H_{12}O_6 + 6\ O_2$$

(Eq. 11.2)

$$3\ O_2 + 2\ I^- \rightarrow 2\ IO_3^-$$

Equation 11.1 shows a highly simplified reaction for photosynthesis, yielding sugar and oxygen gas. Copious amounts of oxygen in this form irritate the tissues of the host organism, causing them to shrivel or close in an attempt to shield their zooxanthellae crop from light. In the presence of iodide, the oxygen is bound into the iodate molecule, which appears to be far less toxic and is probably one of the coping mechanisms available to hermatypic organisms in the wild; this reaction is shown in Eq. 11.2.

Supplements

There are various iodine supplements available, all of them liquids. When it became widely professed throughout the marine aquarium hobby that iodine and iodide were important to the resident organisms, aquarists started experimenting with tincture of iodine, Lugol's solution, and potassium iodide. There are several iodine supplements manufactured specifically for marine aquaria, and

◀ Xenia *sp. seems to thrive in systems with relatively high concentrations of iodine-bearing molecules, but overdosing with an iodine supplement can wipe out an entire marine aquarium in seconds. Nearly every invertebrate in this aquarium "melted" when the iodine concentration suddenly spiked after using a mild oxidizer during a test.*

many are easy to use and have clearly written dosing instructions.

It's very important to note that overdosing these substances can have disastrous effects on an aquarium system; an overdose of iodine can kill beneficial bacteria and destroy sensitive tissue, leading to the rapid demise of the system's inhabitants.

Also, iodine appears to be a biolimiting nutrient for some forms of cyanobacteria, meaning that an elevated iodine concentration in the presence of other required nutrients can encourage the rapid growth of cyanobacterial sheets; this is all the more reason to control the amount of phosphate in the system.

This Xenia *colony has recovered from iodine overdose after six months in optimal chemical, lighting, and water-flow conditions. This system receives iodine supplementation on a weekly basis.*

Test Kits

There are few accurate iodine test kits on the aquarium market, so it's difficult to determine the concentration of iodine without investing in a laboratory-grade test kit. Stick with supplements that contain only iodine, iodide (present as potassium iodide), and deionized water, and add half the manufacturer's suggested dosage until the product's impact may be assessed on the inhabitants, then gradually increase the dosage as necessary. A range of 0.05 to 0.08 mg/L of ionic iodine is acceptable for both fish-only and reef systems.

In Case of Emergency

Should there be a need to rapidly decrease the concentration of iodine in a marine aquarium, there is no

faster way than with one of the aquarium supplements formulated to detoxify chlorine, chloramines, and ammonia. Look specifically for products that smell of sulfur, or rotten eggs. The active ingredient in these products will not only neutralize chlorine, but also iodine and the other elements of the halogen group. It is strongly recommended that a bottle of this solution be kept on hand at all times if Lugol's solution is used in the aquarium; in the unlikely event that the system is overdosed for some reason, quickly adding a few milliliters of the product will neutralize all iodine in the system and could mean the difference between a major catastrophe and a simple scare. Most hobbyists would agree that the few dollars that an 8-oz. bottle of such a product costs are certainly worth the investment.

CHAPTER 12

Iron

Iron, utilized during the production of chloroplasts, is typically a limiting trace element for photosynthetic organisms, the desirable forms in reef aquaria including phytoplankton, micro- and macroalgae, coralline algae, and the symbiotic zooxanthellae living within the tissues of hermatypic invertebrates. Other nutrients that typically encourage algal proliferation, such as phosphate and nitrate, are rarely limiting in marine aquarium systems to the point that the algae are stifled by the absence of adequate concentrations of these substances; rather, iron is often the limiting factor. This is apparent to an aquarist operating an iron-deficient, "low algae" system, who then adds too much of an iron supplement and observes a proliferation of microalgae in the aquarium. In the absence of excessive phosphate and nitrate concentrations, iron addition cannot directly induce algal blooms.

Iron is, however, a very important trace element in reef aquaria, albeit in fairly low concentrations (the natural seawater concentration of iron is approximately 5.5×10^{-5} mg/L). Nevertheless, maintaining the iron concentration at 0.1 to 0.3 mg/L encourages photosynthesis of symbiotic zooxanthellae and other plants in a system, generally without causing rampant growth of microalgae; the higher the rate of photosynthesis taking place, the greater the rate of nutrient uptake, which is a desirable process. All of

▲ *Macroalgae such as this* Halimeda *sp. require adequate available iron in order to produce chlorophyll. In aquaria without large populations of macroalgae, regular water changes and the occasional use of a trace-element supplement containing iron are usually all that is needed to maintain the miniscule required concentration of this element in the system.*

this leads to better growth and improved coloration of the host organisms, and helps curtail chances for uncontrollable growth of filamentous algae.

Supplements

Hobbyists are often unaware of the presence of copious nutrients in their aquaria until they begin using an iron supplement; therefore, when first using an iron supplement in an aquarium system, it's always best to begin by adding one-half (or less) the

manufacturer's recommended dosage for a given volume of water. If the first few weeks of product usage result in an improved appearance of the livestock but no appreciable change in the presence of filamentous algae, the rate of addition may be gradually increased; on the other hand, the hobbyist might decide not to alter the dosage rate that they've already found works with their system, since the only indication of overdosing is the rapid growth of filamentous algae. These algae will overgrow practically anything unable to move, and will smother corals if in great enough mass.

Other problems associated with filamentous algae blooms are the tendency for pH to shift dramatically between day and night, and their direct competition for nutrients with zooxanthellae. If even the initial dose of iron in an aquarium spurs a sudden proliferation of nuisance algae, there is most likely an overabundance of other nutrients such as nitrate and/or phosphate, and steps must be taken to remedy the problem before additional iron supplementation is made.

Test Kits

Formal testing for iron is useful, because there is a thin line between an acceptable concentration of iron in a system and too much. The problem is that the sensitivity of most iron test kits is not less than 0.5 mg/L. Since the hobbyist is trying to maintain the iron concentration in the system in a smaller range than these kits will accurately measure, all that can be done is to test for the presence of iron and be sure that the concentration does not exceed 0.5 mg/L. Alternatively, the hobbyist can reference Appendix V and perform calculations based on the concentration of the iron supplement being used; these calculations will provide an approximate iron concentration.

CHAPTER 13

Phosphate and the Phosphorus Cycle

Phosphorus is a nutrient, a substance (organic or inorganic) that is required and utilized by plants, algae, and phytoplankton for nourishment. In ocean water, inorganic phosphorus (the form needed by photosynthetic organisms such as algae) is present in a very low concentration. Phytoplankton, the major primary producers in the ocean, are affected by the relative presence or absence of inorganic phosphorus, hence it is a biolimiting element.

The Importance of Phosphorus

Most of the information presented in aquarium literature presents only one side of the information on this subject and does not address the actual importance of this element. A basic understanding of the phosphorus cycle and the role that phosphorus plays in an aquatic environment is worth reviewing to understand why phosphorus is essential to all ornamental aquarium inhabitants.

The discussion should begin with the primary producers, which in the context of a marine aquarium will include all photosynthetic organisms. Photosynthetic organisms utilize phosphorus as a component of cell tissue. It is taken up during the process of photosynthesis.

(Eq. 13.1)

$$106\ CO_2 + 122\ H_2O + 16\ HNO_3 + H_3PO_4 \leftrightarrow$$

phosphate utilized

$$(CH_2O)_{106}(NH_3)_{16}H_3PO_4 + 138\ O_2$$

organic matter produced

The transition of phosphorus from an inorganic form to an organic form can be seen in Eq. 13.1. Although it appears to be used in the form of phosphoric acid (H_3PO_4), in reality it is more likely that the hydrogen ions are not utilized; only the phosphate portion (PO_4^{3-}) of the overall molecule is, hence the common approach of using fast-growing macroalgae to remove phosphate from a marine aquarium system. The zooxanthellae residing within the tissues of giant clams, hermatypic corals, and their allies remove a small percentage of the phosphate from solution. This point bears emphasizing: all organisms that are either photosynthetic **or** harbor photosynthetic organisms *require* phosphorus (as phosphate) in the system. We'll set this point aside for the moment in order to discuss organic material.

There are two methods of breaking down organic matter: aerobic and anaerobic. As plant tissue dies and/or is consumed by various aerobic organisms, it is in essence sent in reverse of Eq. 13.1. In other words, instead of phosphate being consumed, it is now *produced*, or rather, liberated.

(Eq. 13.2)

$$\underbrace{(CH_2O)_{106}(NH_3)_{16}H_3PO_4}_{\text{organic matter utilized}} + 138\ O_2 \leftrightarrow 106\ CO_2 + 122\ H_2O + 16\ HNO_3 + \underbrace{H_3PO_4}_{\text{phosphate produced}}$$

Equation 13.2 demonstrates how the decomposition of large amounts of latent organic matter, including dead algae, fish, invertebrates, microbes such as bacteria and fungi, and especially uneaten food, release phosphate and simultaneously decrease the overall concentration of oxygen in a system. This is the process at work in habitats (such as estuaries and other semi-enclosed or fully-enclosed bodies of water) polluted with large concentrations of phosphate, eventually becoming completely inhospitable to aerobic organisms. Since oxygen is being removed from the water very rapidly, aerobic organisms suffocate, die, and become yet another source of organic matter to be broken down.

▲ *The Christmas tree worm,* Spirobranchus *sp., is one of the many invertebrates that require water-borne food, which must be used sparingly to avoid polluting the water.*

As organic matter encounters an environment devoid of oxygen, it must be broken down by anaerobic means. In marine aquarium systems, this process happens in the deep pores of live rock and deep in sand beds. One anaerobic method of organic matter decomposition is sulfate reduction, familiar to anyone who has noticed black areas deep in their live sand beds and has smelled hydrogen sulfide when disturbing these areas. The other method is denitrification. Both processes release phosphate back into the system, as well as ammonia. However, because sulfate reduction also produces sulfide, which then is incorporated into poisonous hydrogen sulfide gas,

it is certainly a less desirable occurrence in an enclosed aquarium system. This is the risk that is run when a sand bed develops anaerobic conditions—hence the strong recommendation to keep the depth of the bed shallow enough to prevent sulfate reduction and/or to employ inhabitants that burrow through the sand, keeping the water in the spaces between the substrate oxygenated and simultaneously consuming organic matter.

Sources of Phosphate

Some of the most common sources of phosphate that pertain to aquarium care are discussed below.

Overfeeding

This topic is discussed at greater length in the chapter pertaining to dissolved and particulate organic matter, but for now let it be said that overfeeding of one or any combination of foods is arguably the single largest cause of phosphate-related problems the hobbyist is likely to face. Feeding the fish and invertebrates is necessary, however care must be taken *not to overfeed* them; doing so is counterproductive to the campaign for success with any aquarium system. In this instance, "overfeeding" implies that food is left to decompose somewhere in the system.

Tap Water

In many instances areas in which copious amounts of fertilizers are used, such as in agricultural regions

An abundance of uneaten food, especially liquid food suspensions and powdered foods, is one of the major contributors to the proliferation of microalgae and cyanobacteria in the home aquarium.

and homes near large public parks, golf courses, and livestock farming operations, have been found to have relatively high concentrations of phosphate in ground and tap water. In general, if unfiltered tap water will be used in a marine aquarium, it's strongly recommended that this water be tested for phosphate, as well as silicate, ammonia, nitrite, nitrate, pH, and alkalinity, just for good measure. Depending on the test results, it may prove beneficial to use filtered water, either by purchasing it from a store or by purchasing a water purification unit and filtering the water as it comes from the tap.

Decomposition of Organic Material

This falls in line with overfeeding, in which excess food is allowed to be broken down by bacteria and/or scavengers in the system; the end

Corky sea fingers, Briareum ashetinum, *benefit from occasional feedings of zooplankton, and uneaten particles are greedily eaten by fishes sharing the same aquarium.*

result is the same: a spike in the amount of phosphate made available due to the remineralization of particulate and dissolved organic matter. If a fish or invertebrate dies, remove it from the aquarium as quickly as possible; the longer this material remains in the aquarium, the more it decomposes, and the greater the effect on water quality as a result.

Use of Low-Grade Activated Carbon

There are numerous types and grades of activated carbon available to aquarium hobbyists. Many of them will release phosphate into the water, a result of leftover phosphoric acid used to create the pores in the raw carbon material. High grades of activated carbon are more expensive than coconut-shell-based grades, but they leach far less phosphate into the system and are therefore the only sensible choice for use in a marine aquarium, if this medium is to be used at all.

A simple method to determine which brand of carbon releases the least phosphate is to take a standard amount of each brand of activated carbon (1 gram, for instance), and immerse it in 4 ounces of purified water. Allow 15 to 20 minutes to pass, then test the water in each cup for phosphate. The point is that activated carbon is used to remove organic material from an aquarium; it should not *contribute* a significant amount of phosphate to the system.

Phosphate in Living Things

Having discussed the cycle, it is now possible to focus on the final destination of all this phosphate and organic material: the tissue of living organisms. Because animals such as fishes and ahermatypic invertebrates only take up phosphate during feeding activities, they are not likely to be a significant phosphate sink in a marine aquarium. Algae, on the other hand, are removing phosphate all the while that photosynthesis is taking place. In a marine aquarium with a high phosphate concentration and abundant iron and nitrogen, prolific and unwanted algae and cyanobacteria growth is practically assured. The whole process is like a loop with a perpetual source of fuel. Phosphate is continually added to the system and assimilated into organic tissue, enabling animals and plants to grow. Because it's typically the goal of every hobbyist to encourage the growth of aquarium inhabitants, no organisms are culled, and therefore no phosphate is ever removed by that means. However, by harvesting algae from a system in which the animals are fed often, phosphate is effectively removed. This is the idea behind the algae turf scrubbers used in waste-water treatment, and more recently in aquarium filtration systems.

The concentration of phosphorus in ocean water is approximately 0.07 mg/L. Only a small fraction of the entire reservoir of aqueous phosphorus is present as a phosphate compound that is easily assimilated by plants, however. It is recommended that the phosphate concentration in a marine aquarium be kept as low as possible, i.e. <0.05 mg/L. It would be extremely difficult to remove all of the phosphate from a marine aquarium (furthermore it would be detrimental to the inhabitants), but keeping the concentration as low as possible will help minimize the likelihood of the problems referred to throughout this chapter. One way to do this is to keep a garden of macroalgae or microalgae in the system, but several manufacturers offer resins and other phosphate-removing filtration media for marine aquarium systems. These products must be placed in an area of high water flow, such as in an overflow or sump, or used in a fluidized-bed media reactor for maximum effectiveness, and should be considered last resorts to deal with phosphate- and organic material-related problems.

Phosphate Adsorption

There are instances where phosphate is adsorbed by porous media, such as the various resins mentioned above, as well as rock and bottom substrate, and is then leached out afterward. This process can be puzzling and very frustrating for hobbyists unfamiliar with it. One mechanism by which live rock and sand absorb and then release phosphate is the temporary incorporation of organic material into and beneath the living biofilm that bacteria create on a porous surface. As mentioned previously, the bacterial population in an aquatic system is driven partly by the abundance of organic material. When an ample supply of this material exists in an aquarium and biolimiting nutrients are abundant, the bacterial population grows very rapidly. When a hobbyist starts seeing the signs of organic overload (typically in the form of rampant growth of filamentous algae throughout the aquarium), it's time to perform a phosphate test on the aquarium water, pinpoint the sources, change the routine, and employ aggressive chemical filtration and frequent partial water changes to try and correct the imbalance. After a period of time, a second phosphate test on the aquarium water will usually indicate that the concentration has decreased substantially from the initial value.

Although the hobbyist may take comfort in the accomplishment and may feel that the problem has been solved, the relief is often temporary. In removing organic material from the aquarium so aggressively, the hobbyist has removed a large percentage of the bacteria's food source, and they begin to die. As the bacteria decompose, the concentration of phosphate in the system rebounds, and the algae that had begun to die back rebound within a few days' time. A third analysis of the water indicates a phosphate concentration in the water as high or higher than was initially recorded. In addition to the sudden decrease in nutrients, decomposition of bacteria in the pores and crevices of live rock and sand depletes the local oxygen concentration in these spaces, causing the death of additional

▲ ***This tricolor* Acropora *frag can grow into a full colony, but not if it is smothered by algae. Maintaining consistently low phosphate levels requires a delicate balance, since phosphate feeds both algae and bacteria, and a sudden decrease in available phosphate can cause a bacteria die-off, which can fuel a new algae bloom.***

bacteria, and the cycle continues until a balance is reached between the amount of nutrients in the system and the bacteria that are left. The hobbyist may need to repeat this procedure several times before the phosphate concentration in the aquarium is consistently immeasurable.

Phosphate Adsorption

The adsorption and subsequent release of phosphate onto/from calcareous particles is another mechanism implicated in this bouncing phosphate scenario. Phosphate tends to form relatively strong bonds with calcium carbonate particles; this reaction is a major sink of phosphate in estuarine environments. The more calcareous sediment that is present in the aquarium system, the greater the amount of phosphate that can be temporarily bound. In a marine aquarium, this phosphate pool should not be dismissed as trivial; in fact, it may contain a very significant amount of phosphate. The factor that determines if and when the phosphate will be released is the ratio between the total quantity of phosphate bound on the particles and the phosphate concentration in the water itself. When the concentration of phosphate in the water suddenly plummets due to the phosphate-

◀ *Soft corals like this leather coral can also be reproduced by fragmentation, and they also need an algae-free environment to survive. Calcareous substrates can be a phosphate sink from which phosphate is released when the aquarist takes steps to reduce the phosphate levels in the tank.*

reduction efforts of the hobbyist, phosphate that is bound to calcareous media will begin to re-enter the water; the signs that this is happening are the same as those mentioned in the previous paragraph. The problem is dealt with in the same fashion described above, also.

Aquaria that have had a persistently high phosphate concentration are the most likely to experience one or both

An invertebrate garden like this one, highlighted by a delicate white stony coral with orange polyps, can be the reward for consistent efforts to keep phosphate levels low in the aquarium.

of these scenarios. Numerous hobbyists have encountered this scenario and solved it (prior to conversation with someone familiar with the process) by discarding all of their live rock and sand and starting over from scratch; this is a very costly, and unnecessary, means of approaching the issue. With time, due effort, and a decrease in the input of organic material to the aquarium, the problem is eventually corrected.

Controlling Phosphate Concentration

As mentioned in the section dealing with calcium supplementation, use of kalkwasser can help control the phosphate concentration through formation of low-solubility calcium-phosphate compounds. However, the physical removal of particulate and dissolved organic matter both before and during decomposition and remineralization of organic material greatly helps the hobbyist avoid phosphate-related problems, and it is for this reason that every marine aquarium stands to benefit from the use of efficient protein skimming, arguably the hobbyist's best ally in the struggle to minimize latent organic material present in the system.

Testing

There are many phosphate test kits available to marine aquarium hobbyists. Testing may be performed on a weekly to bi-weekly basis, depending on whether or not the hobbyist feels that it's warranted. In general, the sudden emergence of any type of cyanobacteria or filamentous algae in an aquarium that previously appeared free of these organisms is an indication that the phosphate concentration is higher than recommended.

CHAPTER 14

Dissolved and Particulate Organic Matter

The abundance of organic matter, whether it is dissolved or particulate in form, greatly impacts the appearance of a marine aquarium as well as the overall health of the inhabitants. It is inevitable and normal that dissolved organic matter (DOM) and/or particulate organic matter (POM) exist in the system; the main points of interest are the concentration and relative abundance of DOM and POM, and the rate at which they are being broken down, or remineralized, into their constituents—mainly carbon, hydrogen, nitrogen, oxygen, phosphorus, and sulfur. Of these elements, nitrogen and phosphorus, as nutrients, and the concentrations of molecules into which they become incorporated—such as ammonia, nitrite, and nitrate in the case of nitrogen, and phosphate in the case of phosphorus—are a good indication of the overall health and stability of the biological community in an aquarium, and suggest whether alternative or additional means of filtration may be required. In natural seawater, nitrogen and phosphorus are in the lowest abundance relative to the other elements mentioned, and so limit the productivity of the organisms responsible for both producing and breaking down organic matter, namely phytoplankton and bacteria, respectively.

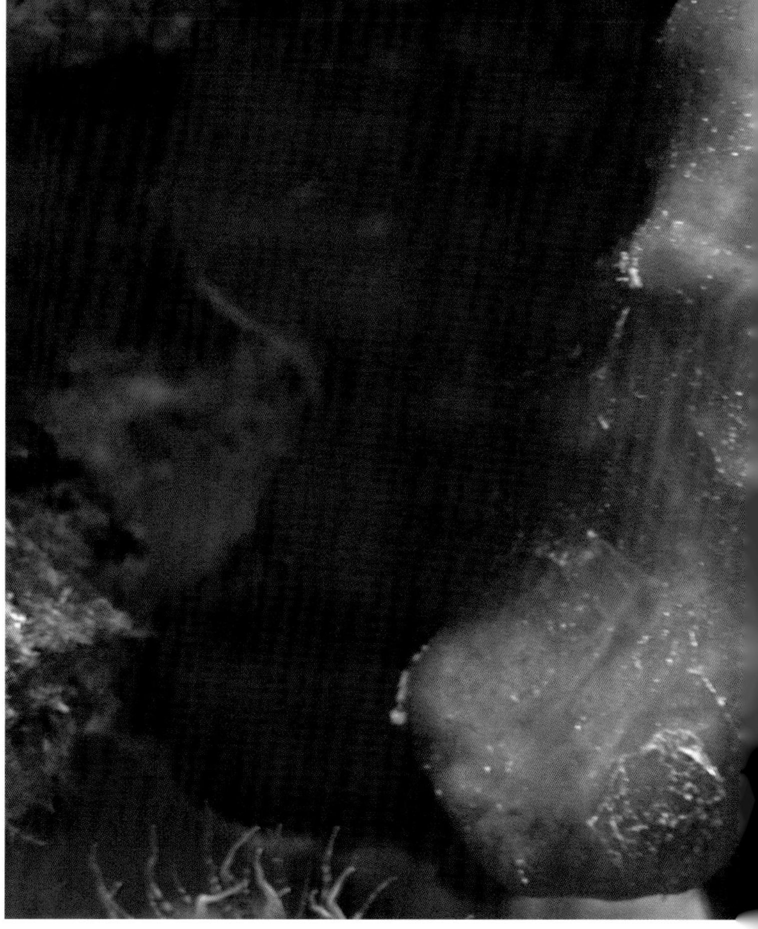

The Cycle

The complete process of organic matter production and destruction is a continuous cycle. Plants and algae take up the elements of organic matter and create tissue. When eaten by other organisms, their body constituents are either incorporated into the grazing organisms' tissues or are excreted, with the process continuing on through the food chain. Bacteria and other microbes then break down dead tissue and fecal material, and the nitrogen and phosphorus are released back into the water to re-enter the cycle, and the process begins anew. Most tropical waters are relatively nutrient-poor and therefore support very little phytoplankton growth as compared to habitats in higher latitudes and in areas where nutrient-rich water is upwelling from the depths.

In a marine aquarium, excess dissolved nitrogen and phosphorus are naturally utilized by sessile forms of algae, including those living within the tissues of host invertebrates, by bacteria, and by cyanobacteria. While the two former groups are encouraged to thrive, the latter group is not. The key to limiting cyanobacterial growth is to remove excessive organic matter from the system before it's broken down. The use of efficient protein skimming, activated carbon, organic adsorption resins, and water changes helps facilitate this process.

Sponges such as this red ball sponge, Pseudaxinella reticulata, *require food, typically in the form of phytoplankton, if they are to remain healthy and growing. Attempts to provide this food, no matter how noble the hobbyist's intentions are, should begin on a "minimalist" basis, starting out with a fraction of the manufacturer's recommended dosage and then moving up from there as the aquarium adapts to the higher-than-average concentration of dissolved and particulate organic matter present in liquid food suspensions. Incidentally, sponges also require some form of soluble silica with which to create spongin tissue for continued growth. Trace impurities in some supplements (calcium hydroxide is a good example) tend to provide all the silica needed.*

Overfeeding

The concentration of particulate and dissolved organic material in a system can become excessive if it's overfed and none of those removal mechanisms are employed. Overfeeding is not just limited to fish food; the overuse of invertebrate food supplements can quickly overload an aquarium with organic material and encourage proliferation of cyanobacteria and filamentous algae.

When beginning the use of such a product, it is strongly recommended to dose it no more than two to three times a week at half the manufacturer's recommended dosage for the first month or so; this will enable the biological filtration to ramp up gradually and deal with the increasing amount of organic material without contributing to a significant drop in redox potential. After the first month has passed, slowly increase the

▲ *The many species of burrowing, scavenging gastropods that frequent marine aquaria help prevent a build-up of latent organic matter and are a crucial part of a balanced system.*

dosing frequency if it seems warranted. Delivery of the food suspension (usually containing various species of plankton) is most efficient by target feeding, which makes use of a long pipette to squirt food into the water up-current from the invertebrate being fed; do not squirt a food suspension directly onto the animal, as the chemical composition of the product may irritate sensitive tissues. Feeding in this manner, with the suspension entering the water two to three inches from the animal, allows it to take the particles in naturally and wastes far less food than broadcast feeding (e.g., indiscriminately pouring a capful of the product into a stream of water from a pump).

Protein Skimming

Protein skimming is perhaps the most widely employed—and most effective—means of removing organic material from marine aquarium water. An efficient protein skimmer, properly matched to the volume of water in the complete aquarium system (taking into account the water in the display, sump, and refugium if applicable), is the first and best line of defense against problems caused by excess organics in the system.

Activated Carbon and Absorption Resins

Essentially, one can think of activated carbon and organic adsorption resin beads as being porous, and therefore sponge-like in a way. The sizes of pores in each resin bead and piece of activated carbon enable the removal of dissolved substances from water as it is pumped through beds or bags of these media. There are various grades of activated carbon available to aquarium hobbyists. Regardless of how they're classified by the manufacturer, the best products leach little to no phosphate and aren't made of coconut shells. Disregard the grade designation assigned by the manufacturer and inquire of them as to whether or not the carbon is NSF certified or approved, indicating that it's safe for use in drinking water and food-grade applications.

Preventing Problems

The best defense against a build-up of organic material is a good offense. Most hobbyists would do well to keep a properly sized protein skimmer running at all times in their marine aquaria, and all hobbyists should change a percentage of the water every seven to ten days and not overfeed the livestock. An ORP meter, discussed in detail in the next chapter, can provide a general picture of the overall rate of organic material input and breakdown in a system and is a powerful ally in the effort to keep a marine aquarium system balanced and healthy.

CHAPTER 15

Redox, or Oxidation-Reduction Potential (ORP)

Another name for this chapter could have been "ORP: The Marine Aquarium Early Warning System." A more complete definition of **oxidation-reduction potential (ORP)** will follow, however for now the term may be broadly defined as the ability, hence *potential*, of the system to break down organic matter. To understand how this is possible, the complex nature of redox chemistry must be explored in some detail. Measurement of oxidation-reduction potential can be an invaluable method of determining the overall health of an aquarium system, but *only* if the hobbyist understands how to quantify an ORP reading. That might seem to go without saying, but experience has illustrated that many hobbyists using ORP meters don't fully understand *what* they are measuring, and *why*.

Redox Reaction

An oxidation-reduction, or redox, reaction may be more formally defined as a combination of reactions in which atoms and molecules gain and lose electrons. To bring this into the context of aquaria, these reactions are utilized by organisms to form energy; organic material (as the electron donor) and oxygen, nitrate, or sulfate (as the electron acceptors, or oxidizing agents) are the requirements for heterotrophic organisms, whereas photosynthetic organisms, in the presence of the proper light, employ water as the electron donor and inorganic carbon as the electron acceptor. These

Daily fluctuations in the ORP reading are normal in marine aquaria, and typically coincide with changes in the activity levels of aquarium inhabitants, feeding events, and the rate of production and uptake of organic material as a result of photosynthesis. The loss of life in an aquarium will also influence ORP.

reactions consume and produce organic material, respectively. Additionally, ozone, produced by an ozonator and injected into a protein skimmer or other semi-enclosed reaction vessel as needed, may be employed by the hobbyist as a powerful oxidizing agent to help minimize the abundance of organic material in the system.

All of this may seem complicated, and in all honesty, it is. That being the case, several of the reactions will not be discussed in detail, however the process will be briefly reviewed to provide a basic understanding of what ORP entails. For an example, consider organic matter as an electron donor and oxygen and nitrate as electron acceptors; this is the method of energy production for animals and many microbes.

There is often an abundance of organic matter in a typical marine aquarium. Even with efficient protein skimming, water changes, and the use of organic removing resins, the concentration of particulate and dissolved organic matter is probably far greater in an average reef aquarium than in the waters overlying a natural reef. Redox reactions must take place in order for a reef to operate smoothly, regardless of whether it exists in nature or the hobbyist's home. It is through these reactions that organic matter is broken down into its components and recycled into the system to play important roles in water chemistry and be used in metabolic processes. Two examples of redox reactions were demonstrated in Eqs. 7.2 and 13.2. In these two reactions, nitrate and oxygen are reduced by gaining electrons from organic matter[1]. In turn, the organic matter is broken down to an extent. To summarize, organic matter is oxidized, and oxygen and nitrate are reduced. Using the impact that these reactions have on aquatic environments as determining criteria, it may be stated that these are the two most important reduction reactions to take place both in a reef aquarium and a natural reef.

Oxidation-Reduction Potential

This leads to the topic of ORP. Technically, ORP is a measurement of the transfer of electrons between a negative and positive cell, and hence has units of volts (usually millivolts). The higher the millivolts read, the higher the system's potential for breaking down organic matter ("higher" being a relative term). The key to gauging the importance of an ORP reading is therefore to monitor the ORP of the aquarium over a prolonged period of time. To illustrate this concept with an example, consider an aquarium in which the ORP consistently remains within a range of 340 to 370 mV. Then one morning the ORP reads 175 mV. The likely cause is the remineralization of abundant organic material by heterotrophic bacteria, consuming the oxidizing agents in solution at a greater rate than usual. In short, something is probably dead and decomposing in an inaccessible corner of the aquarium, as Murphy's

[1] Electrons have a negative electrical charge, and so gaining an electron actually is a reduction in the electron acceptor's overall charge.

Law dictates. Aquarium inhabitants often won't look their best under such conditions due to the increasing concentration of nitrogenous waste in the water. One method that may be employed to help avert long-term negative impacts on the remaining inhabitants is to utilize an ORP controller and ozone unit in conjunction with an efficient protein skimmer.

Ozone

Ozone (O_3) is a molecule composed of three oxygen atoms; this is unusual under most circumstances in nature, as oxygen predominantly exists as O_2, not O_3. In nature, ozone is formed by ultraviolet light (from the sun) passing through an oxygen molecule, liberating one of the atoms in a process known as photolysis. As shown in Eq. 15.1, ozone is also created by passing an electrical current through oxygen in the gaseous state, liberating oxygen atoms, and is the method employed in ozonators. In both cases, the free oxygen atom forms a weak bond when it collides with a molecule of oxygen. The nature of this weak bond is what dictates the rate of ozone decay and the extent to which it will affect different substances.

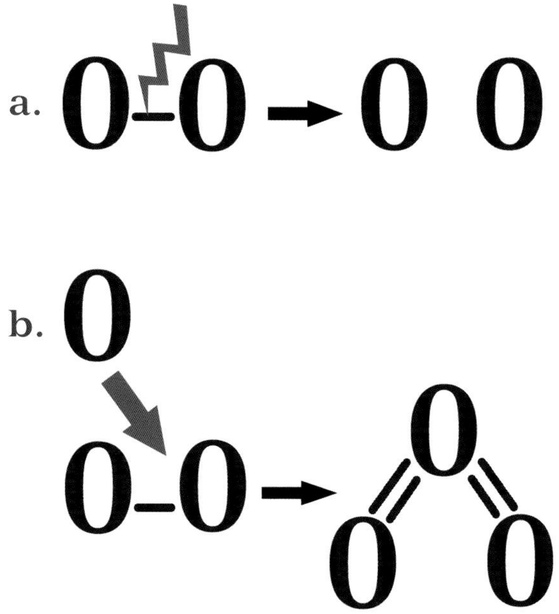

▲ ***This figure represents the formation of ozone: a. the dissociation of an oxygen molecule O_2 by high energy (UV or electricity) into two oxygen atoms by breaking a very strong double bond; b. the collision of a free oxygen atom with an oxygen molecule produces a molecule of ozone O_3. The oxygen atoms in this molecule are bound by a single bond and a shared bond, which gives the molecule its instability.***

(Eq. 15.1)
$$O_2 + O \rightarrow O_3$$

An ozone molecule has no net electrical charge, but it can obtain up to two electrons from another source, making it a strong oxidant. Though the chemical structure of the material being acted upon by ozone will dictate the rate of oxidation, it can generally be stated that ozone will readily react with organic matter, regardless of whether it's incorporated into living or dead tissue, breaking it down in the process. It is in this way that ozone is used to reduce the concentration of organic matter, including microbes such as bacteria and viruses, in aquarium systems.

An ozonator produces ozone, which is then injected into the system in a semi-closed reaction vessel (such as a protein skimmer) to react with organic material with which it comes into contact. The use of a continuous ORP monitor/controller triggers the ozonator to release ozone into the system (preferably the skimmer) only as needed, maintaining a user-determined minimum ORP.

Because ozone is so powerful an oxidant, very little is required to service even the largest aquaria. A properly sized ozonator and a sensible approach to injection will minimize the amount of ozone that escapes into the sump or aquarium system. The primary danger of allowing excess ozone to pass freely into the main aquarium is irritation of the livestock's sensitive tissues[2]. It is for this reason that protein skimmers utilizing ozone are sometimes fitted with activated carbon filters, which remove excess ozone before it escapes into the aquarium and local atmosphere.

See the following example of how to translate the readings provided by an ORP meter; for the aquarium in question, assume that it's a well-stocked reef with several relatively small fish. The chart follows a two-day period for the sake of demonstrating the common variability in ORP.

[2] Lung irritation of nearby people or animals would only be likely under extreme circumstances and is exceedingly improbable.

Table 15.1 ORP Changes Over Two Days

Time	ORP Reading	Action	Notes
8 a.m.	403	Actinic lights switch on.	ORP is often highest just before lights come on.
10 a.m.	398	Daylights switch on.	Livestock has begun grazing and producing waste.
12 p.m.	395	Livestock is fed.	Amount of food added to aquarium will impact severity of ORP change.
2 p.m.	375	None	ORP decreases due to breakdown of organics from food.
4 p.m.	385	None	ORP has begun to rebound as organic materials are broken down.
6 p.m.	350	Daylights switch off.	A fish has been discovered to be missing.
8 p.m.	240	Actinic lights switch off.	You discover the fish, dead and being consumed by various livestock.
10 p.m.	242	None	ORP has begun to rebound as fish is consumed.
8 a.m.	390	Actinic lights switch on.	ORP has returned to normal as organic matter has been reduced.
10 a.m.	395	Daylights switch on.	Livestock has begun grazing and producing waste.
12 p.m.	395	Livestock is fed.	Amount of food added to aquarium will impact severity of ORP change.
2 p.m.	380	None	ORP decreases due to breakdown of organics from food.
4 p.m.	385	None	ORP has begun to rebound as organic materials are broken down.
6 p.m.	388	Daylights switch off.	ORP continues to gradually increase as organic material is further oxidized.
8 p.m.	387	Actinic lights switch off.	Everything in the system appears normal, ORP is steady.
10 p.m.	392	None	Fish are asleep, nocturnal invertebrates are out feeding and scavenging.
8 a.m.	404	Actinic lights switch on.	Once again, ORP is highest at this point of the light cycle.

▲ *Large-polyp stony corals are for many hobbyists difficult to maintain in captivity over long periods of time. So many factors can contribute to the success or failure with particular species that it often takes several attempts to maintain an organism or colony alive long term. Monitoring ORP provides an early warning system for problems that can arise, giving the aquarist time to react before conditions become critical.*

This example illustrates the fact that ORP varies during the course of the day, and that these variations are all an indicator of the amount of latent organic material in the system that has yet to be broken down relative to what is *normally* in the system. It is in this manner that an ORP meter can be used to alert the hobbyist to the overall health of the system relative to that at other points in time. ORP is normally highest in the morning just prior to the lights coming on for the day, which interestingly enough coincides with the time at which pH in the system is lowest. After the lights have been on for an hour or so, the ORP will have begun to drop slightly, largely due to the morning

routine of fish and invertebrates that have woken up and are beginning to feed and excrete. Typically, ORP throughout the rest of the day will stay relatively constant, to within ±30 mV, unless the concentration of decaying organic material in the system increases significantly; overfeeding and/or the death of livestock or the bacterial bed are common causes of a rapid decrease in ORP, as the example illustrates.

Remineralization

To illustrate another aspect of aquarium water chemistry in which knowing the ORP can be enlightening, consider the impact of the remineralization of particulate organic matter on trace elements. When a relatively low amount of organic material is being oxidized and the ORP is consequently high, the resultant release of any adsorbed trace elements into the system is low. As ORP decreases due to an increasing rate of organic material oxidation, however, the release of trace elements increases, the extent to which this occurs being dependent upon the enrichment of these elements in the tissues being broken down. Therefore, it is often the case that as ORP decreases, the amount of trace elements entering the system is likely to be higher than at other times, though there is no direct numerical relationship between these two processes. This process is described merely to demonstrate that ORP can have more benefits than those outwardly apparent, if the hobbyist understands how to interpret the readings.

Tongue coral, another of the large-polyp stony species that can sometimes be difficult to maintain over long periods of time. Hobbyists interested in attempting to keep one of these corals are advised to seek the guidance of other hobbyists in their local area that can offer some first-hand, credible, and practical guidance with care requirements. ORP monitoring can be especially helpful with difficult species.

Controlling ORP

Hobbyists determined to keep the amount of latent dissolved and particulate organic material as low as is currently possible in their aquaria will find an ORP controller and ozonator to be powerful tools for this purpose. By no means are these systems an absolute requirement for the maintenance of a successful aquarium system; an efficient protein skimmer will perform most of the duties of free-organic removal in the vast majority of aquaria maintained by hobbyists. The use of the ORP meter alone (without the ozonator) can be a very useful tool to provide an impression of overall system health. The meter can pay for itself in terms of helping save the lives of inhabitants that could otherwise be lost should something in the system go wrong.

CHAPTER 16

Silicon, Silica, and Silicate

References to the chemistry of silicon tend to interchange back and forth between nomenclature confusingly, creating a need to define the terms for readers:

Silicon is the name given to the basic element, Si. Silicon is the most abundant element in the Earth's crust, accounting for over 28% of it by weight.

Silica is the name given to silicon dioxide, SiO_2. It is often used as a catch-all term to describe silicon-bearing molecules.

Silicate is the name given to metal oxides of silica, such as sodium silicate, Na_2SiO_3; for this reason, silicates are classified as salts.

Silicon binds with other elements to form various species of silica and silicate. The concentrations of soluble silica molecules are important to marine aquarium hobbyists primarily because they influence (and limit) the growth of diatoms; these soluble molecules are also termed "reactive" and are nutrients. Solubility is directly proportional to the amount of water bound in the molecules; the more water present, the greater the solubility. In most waters, the predominant form of dissolved silica is monosilicic acid (H_4SiO_4), which incorporates two water molecules and surrounds itself with an additional four, making a total of six.

Colloids and Particles

There are two other forms in which

▲ *This pink sponge,* Darwinella mulleri, *will benefit from the presence of trace amounts of soluble silica in the aquarium.*

silica molecules may exist: colloidal and particulate. Colloidal silica is that which has become bound with multiple additional silica molecules, organic material, or complex inorganic molecules (typically featuring calcium). In this form, it remains suspended in solution and is not reactive. Suspended silica is that which exists in a crystalline structure, such as quartz sand; as with colloidal silica, it is not available for bio-uptake in this form.

The Danger of Silica

Dissolved silica ranks high on the list of substances that are the bane of marine aquarium hobbyists. Its presence in a marine aquarium encourages the growth of diatoms, a type of phytoplankton that secrete hydrated silica (also known as biogenic silica, opal, or opaline silica) to form their skeletal structures. In a marine aquarium, diatoms may appear as a dusty or stringy, golden-brown coating on rock, sand, or viewing panes. Diatoms don't constitute any threat to the livestock; they simply detract from the appearance of the system.

Diatoms

In the open ocean, diatoms take in nutrients more rapidly than any other group of phytoplankton. The concentration of dissolved silica in seawater limits their productivity (hence their rates of growth and reproduction), and therefore is directly linked to overall marine productivity. In areas where sufficient dissolved silicate exists, some other nutrient, such as iron, often becomes the limiting factor in diatom productivity.

Diatoms are able to reproduce sexually and through asexual fission. In the latter case, a parent diatom essentially splits in two. Each half then secretes another half to create a whole diatom. Once the secretion is complete, the diatom is ready for asexual reproduction again. This process continues in a logarithmic fashion described by 2^n, where n is the number of generations: one diatom becomes 2, then 4, 8, 16, 32, 64, 128, 256, 512, 1,024, 2,048, etc. By the twentieth generation the number is over a million. Therefore, a diatom bloom can occur quite rapidly if the concentration of dissolved silica suddenly increases for some reason.

Since with each progressive division smaller organisms are created, the average physical size of the diatoms decreases with time, eventually due to the sheer diminutive size of the diatoms they reach a stage in which sexual reproduction becomes necessary. The fertilized eggs produce large diatoms, and the process outlined above repeats itself. In the context of marine aquarium care, diatoms may be thought of as a water quality indicator of sorts; a modest to heavy growth of diatoms in the aquarium indicates that the concentration of dissolved silica is higher than desirable.

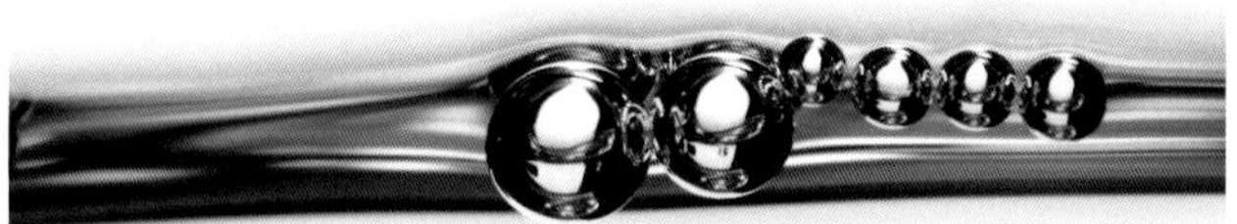

Silica for Sponges

Generally, silica present in the water used to make an aquarium's salt water or in impurities in the synthetic salt mix itself, as well as in supplements, provides adequate silica for the growth of sponges. However, hobbyists may choose to supplement aquaria housing dense sponge populations with sodium metasilicate to increase growth rates.

Radiolarians and Sponges

Two other groups of organisms that utilize dissolved silica are radiolarians, a type of zooplankton that are unlikely to be found in closed aquarium systems in any significant density, and sponges. Sponges often grow more rapidly when adequate dissolved silica is present than when it's lacking; this is due, at least in part, to the fact that many sponges use silica (and calcium carbonate) to form spicules that make up a sort of skeletal structure. Aquaria that are filled and topped off with unpurified tap water often house large numbers of small, white, pineapple- or vase-shaped sponges (the purse sponge *Scypha barbadensis*). To an extent, these organisms may act as a biological controller of dissolved silica, and help limit the growth of diatoms on some order of magnitude.

Sources of Silicon

Some of the most common sources of dissolved silicon that pertain to aquarium care are discussed below.

Tap Water

Tap water is probably the greatest source of dissolved silica in aquarium circles. Some regions of the United States (such as in California and the Great Basin) have relatively high concentrations of dissolved silica naturally occurring in the aquifers. In addition, many municipal water companies across the country add water glass, which is aqueous sodium silicate (Na_2SiO_3), potassium silicate (K_2SiO_3), or a mixture of the two, to their systems to coat the insides of pipes and protect them from corrosion. Hobbyists with measurable concentrations of dissolved silica in their tap water are advised to purify it prior to using it in marine aquaria. Some of the high-silicate-removal reverse osmosis membranes on the market are able to effectively remove up to 99.5% of the dissolved silica from solution, making them the most effective means of preventative maintenance; by comparison, traditional cellulose-triacetate and thin-film composite membranes may remove less than 90% of dissolved silica. Refer to the chapter on tap water purification for detailed explanations of reverse osmosis and deionization processes.

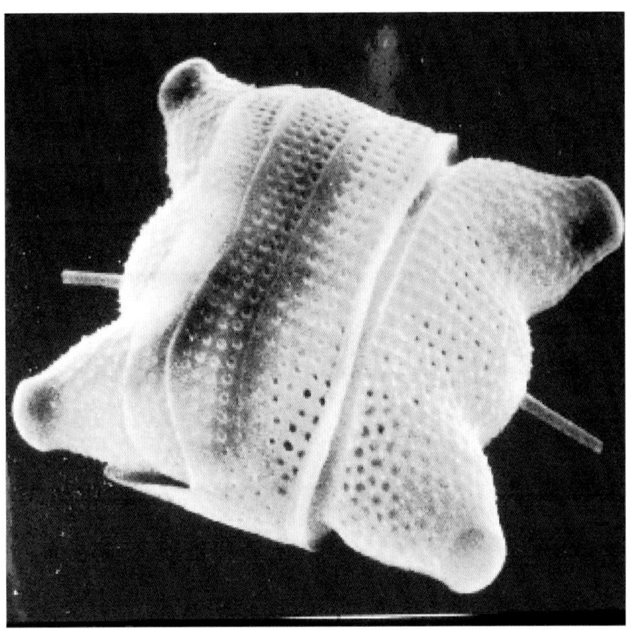

▲ *At the microscopic level the tiny openings in the silicate skeleton of a diatom are quite apparent. It is these openings that make diatom skeletons such an effective filter medium, but a water polishing filter should never be used in a marine tank unless a diatom bloom is desired, as it is when culturing certain diatom grazers.*

Synthetic Sea Salt Blends

Many synthetic sea salt blends contain trace amounts of soluble silica, which is presumably a factor of the purity of raw materials used; a salt blend composed primarily of low-grade raw materials is much more likely to contain relatively high concentrations of soluble silica (as well as other contaminants). When an aquarium is first filled with seawater (regardless of whether or not the fresh water used has been purified), a diatom bloom may occur as the abundance of dissolved silica and other nutrients allows. The use of a premium salt blend and purified water minimizes the likelihood that subsequent blooms will occur. In the event that unfiltered water and/or a

▲ ***High calcium levels fuel the growth of coral skeletons such are formed by* Acropora. *High silicon levels fuel the growth of unwanted diatoms.***

lower-grade salt blend are used, a perpetual problem with keeping diatoms at bay may be experienced; the determining factors are the concentration of soluble silica in the blend and whether or not conditions in the aquaria are conducive to diatom growth. In this event, changing water will simply provide more silica for the diatom growth and reproduction cycle. This is all the more reason to do some research into the quality of numerous brands of salt before committing to using one.

Recurrent problems with diatoms that appear to be related to performing water changes are strong grounds for testing aquarium water and a sample of freshly prepared seawater for silicate. If either indicates an excessive concentration, steps must be taken to correct the problem.

Sandbox, Pool, or Playground Sand

Sand used in children's play areas or in swimming pool filters, as well as most sand obtained along temperate beaches, is largely composed of mineral silica, typically quartz (which is largely insoluble in seawater under average temperature and pressure), with much of the remainder being soluble silica. Because aquarium water is undersaturated with respect to silica, the use of such sand will encourage the growth and reproduction of diatoms. Therefore, it is wise to avoid the use of this type of sand in any marine aquarium.

Diatom Filters

Avoid the temptation to use a diatom filter to "polish" the water in a marine aquarium; this is a guaranteed means of introducing silica. The filter medium itself is nothing more than dead diatoms, which are sucked into a pleated screen by a pump. Aquarium water is forced to flow through this filter, and the resultant tiny spaces between the diatoms remove most particulate matter (including free-swimming ectoparasites) from the water column. During the process, diatoms are dissolving and being broken down into smaller fragments during the operation of the filter, loading the system with dissolved silica. It's therefore logical to conclude that diatom filters have no place in a marine aquarium.

Testing

Performing a formal test to determine the dissolved silica concentration in the marine aquarium is typically only necessary when a sudden or perpetual presence of diatoms is experienced. If a large water change is performed and the beginnings of a diatom bloom appear in the aquarium within the next day or two, the presence of silica in the aquarium will be confirmed. It can be removed by various chemical filtration media and by water changes with seawater free of silica.

Silica Loss

As an aside, it's interesting to note that one of the means in which silica is lost from aquatic systems is through the formation of largely insoluble minerals. This process occurs when dissolved silica interacts with multivalent cations, such as magnesium, calcium, and various trace elements, precipitating and making both the silica and metal unavailable for bio-uptake. The strong bonds formed in these reactions are stable for lengthy periods of time. That being the case, a percentage of dissolved silica is likely removed from marine aquaria due to the high concentrations of magnesium and calcium in the water. Conversely, the presence of these ions in water slows the dissolution of particulate silica.

CHAPTER 17

Trace Elements

As discussed in Chapter 1, trace elements are defined as those elements occurring at a concentration of less than 1 ppb by weight. Trace elements collectively constitute a very minute fraction (approximately 0.0005% by weight) of the total dissolved substances in seawater. Interestingly, 52 of the 77 elements that naturally occur in seawater are trace elements. Thirty-one of the trace elements are affected by biological and chemical processes (non-conservative); 13 of these exhibit behavior suggesting that they are nutrients, with the remainder undergoing depletion (due to incorporation into tissue and skeletal material via chemical processes) in surface waters. Figures 17.1 and 17.2 list these elements.

Many trace elements are important to a number of metabolic (more

Figure 17.1. Trace Elements Exhibiting Nutrient-Type Behavior
Beryllium
Phosphorus
Chromium
Nickel
Copper
Zinc
Germanium
Arsenic
Selenium
Silver
Cadmium
Iodine
Barium

Figure 17.2. Trace Elements Exhibiting Surface Depletion
Scandium
Vanadium
Iron
Cobalt
Lanthanum
Cerium
Praseodymium
Neodymium
Samarium
Europium
Gadolinium
Terbium
Dysprosium
Holmium
Erbium
Thulium
Ytterbium
Lutetium

specifically, enzymatic[1]) and vitamin synthesis reactions for plants and animals alike; additionally, they may influence pigmentation, and therefore coloration, of various organisms. Again, the concept of biolimitation applies to trace elements, as many of them may be required in the presence of other elements or substances in order for some specific biological reaction to occur. This underscores the point that trace elements are indeed important to many biological processes in the marine environment, and warrants use of a salt and/or supplement containing trace elements in marine aquaria on that basis alone. Oceanographers refer to the trace elements that influence biological activity as essential.

[1] Enzymatic reactions include the metabolism of sugars and proteins, as well as photosynthesis. Thus, it may be stated that certain trace metals are very important to marine life.

◀ *The extended feeding tentacles of this coral remind us that corals do not live by light alone. This is not to say that they can't survive for weeks, months, or perhaps even years without supplemental feeding, but it makes no sense to expend the considerable effort required to attain and maintain the water chemistry parameters required by these and other marine organisms, only to* not *feed them when they clearly stand to benefit from the presence of the appropriate types of prey. Similarly, although the benefits of trace mineral supplementation are not well documented, it makes sense to concern yourself with the potential for deficiencies in trace elements in your aquarium.*

The elements listed in figures 17.1 and 17.2 are ultimately those that hobbyists should be interested in supplementing to marine aquaria. Other trace elements exhibit conservative behavior, indicating that they are not utilized in any appreciable quantity by marine organisms, and therefore are essentially unnecessary in marine aquaria. This statement can be made based upon the fact that since such a small percentage of the total dissolved substances in seawater are attributable to trace elements, excluding those that are apparently not needed will have no appreciable impact on the health or appearance of the livestock, nor will their absence significantly impact water chemistry. This has a major implication for the use of trace element supplements in marine aquaria.

Heavy Metals

Heavy metals are those trace elements with an atomic weight greater than 20 atomic mass units

▲ ***This small reef aquarium is no different from systems of several hundred or thousand gallons in terms of the inhabitants' requirements for biologically important trace elements.***

(amu). The periodic table of the elements presented in Appendix I illustrates the elements widely considered by chemists to be heavy metals. Heavy metals are rapidly taken up by living organisms and can be toxic to marine organisms in very small concentrations. The concentrations and chemical forms in which these elements are present in an aquarium system can have a significant impact on the livestock; if they are in an organic or methylated form, the elements pass easily through cell membranes and into the tissue of exposed organisms. This poses significant risk not only to aquarium inhabitants but also to hobbyists handling the material.

Note that certain heavy metals are *required* for normal functioning by aquatic life in some miniscule concentration. However, there is a point at which the concentrations of all trace elements become toxic. In the past few decades, much has been discussed about the dumping of heavy metals (particularly mercury) in to rivers, bays, and estuaries. The general path that many of these metals follow is easy to explain:

- A percentage of the metals in water will bind with organic matter.

- Much of the organic matter will be removed from the aquatic system by filter feeders and detrivores, which make up the diet of many predatory, progressively larger fishes and invertebrates, further enriching the organisms with heavy metals at each step in the food chain; this process is termed biomagnification.

- Because it's not an easy matter to purge a body of these elements, they remain there and accrue with time and continued intake; this building-up process is appropriately termed bioaccumulation.

The effects of bioaccumulation are most pronounced in apex predators, who reside at the top of the food chain. This is illustrated by the high concentrations of toxic mercury in table fishes such as tuna, swordfish, and bluefish, and the associated warnings to limit daily intake of these groups of fishes.

Trace Element Levels

The abundance of trace elements in seawater is largely controlled by two factors: bio-uptake by marine organisms (primarily phytoplankton), and the adsorption of trace elements or their ion pairs onto organic and inorganic particulate materials. In marine aquaria, the presence of macroalgae, microalgae, cyanobacteria, and large amounts of dissolved and particulate organic matter minimize the percentage of trace elements available to ornamental inhabitants. Aquaria meeting any or all of these criteria generally require greater trace element supplementation than those aquaria maintained with no appreciable growth of algae or

▲ *Trace element supplementation may be performed on a regular basis, or the hobbyist may choose to rely on trace element addition from regular water changes to satisfy an aquarium's needs.*

cyanobacteria (such aquaria are likely to have little latent organic matter).

It is the relatively high bioavailability of organic forms of trace elements and heavy metals that has lead to their wide spread use in aquarium supplements; metals bound with EDTA or gluconate are perfect examples. These are not necessarily undesirable methods of delivering trace elements; in fact, without these organic forms, the effectiveness of these supplements would be decreased dramatically in some cases, as many trace elements would readily oxidize in seawater upon addition to the aquarium, making them unavailable to inhabitants. It's mainly for this purpose that using chelated trace elements in aquaria can be sensible, so long as they are not overdosed.

Do Not Eat or Drink

Warnings on the labels of many aquarium products state: "For use on ornamental fishes only. Not to be used on fishes meant for human consumption," or something similar. There are several reasons that these warnings should appear on such a label. For instance, ingredients used may not be FDA-approved for use in food (the ingredients may not even be available in food grade). A hobbyist has no way of effectively measuring or controlling the concentration of trace elements in his or her aquarium. The FDA and American Pet Product Manufacturers Association (APPMA) came to an agreement by which medications containing antibiotics and carcinogenic dyes, and destined for use in aquaculture, would be labeled as noted. To avoid further conflict with the FDA, APPMA decided to request that manufacturers of aquarium supplements list this warning on their labels. These warnings indicate that a manufacturer is both responsible and conscientious of important aspects of aquatic chemistry.

Supplementation

Most trace element supplements available to hobbyists appear to contain a random mixture of trace elements with concentrations that don't seem to fit any purpose; additionally, many of these products contain major and minor elements in addition to trace elements. If such a product contains calcium and strontium, for example, it makes the hobbyist's job of calculating the dosage required to maintain the desired concentrations of those elements more difficult; furthermore, these are clearly not trace elements, so the product is by definition not what it claims to be. Perhaps this is splitting hairs; it's difficult to say. At any rate, preference should be shown to solutions that contain as many of the non-conservative trace elements as possible in the proper ratios to one another; the presence of conservative trace elements in the solution is undesirable but probably a reality with most products, at least at the present time.

Diet

Some hobbyists maintain that

▲ ***Many trace elements are required for proper biological and neurological functioning; regular supplementation of these elements is therefore necessary for continued health of aquarium inhabitants.***

organisms get all of the trace elements they need by eating a varied diet; intrinsically, this depends entirely upon what the animals are eating, and it is exceedingly unlikely that the elements identified as being important to biological processes are all present in prepared foods. If regular water changes are performed using a salt blend containing the required trace elements, the need to supplement with a trace element solution diminishes substantially. Realistically, few aquarists change water as frequently as they probably ought to, so dosing a trace element supplement is likely to be beneficial to aquarium inhabitants, but it is for the most part a matter of blind supplementation, with faith in the manufacturer's claims and recommendations, unless full and accurate disclosure of the constituent elements and their concentrations is provided. In order to maintain relatively constant concentrations of trace elements in an aquarium system, the product should be added daily instead of once weekly or bi-weekly. To do this, simply divide the recommended weekly dosage into seven and add one part to the system each day.

Overdosing

Though trace elements are essential in all marine aquaria, the gross overdosing of a trace element supplement can be harmful to aquarium inhabitants; once the threshold concentration of a particular element has been reached in the tissues of an organism, the result is interference with metabolic and neurological function, and in extreme cases death. For the marine aquarium hobbyist, there are no economical—and in some cases reliable—methods to determine the concentrations of many trace elements present in seawater; therefore it's not possible to get an accurate idea of the relative concentrations of these substances in an aquarium. The problem this creates is simply not knowing how much of the product to use, particularly when the ingredients include conservative elements that will gradually accumulate in the system.

Aqueous trace elements are made unavailable in marine aquaria largely by adsorption to particulate organic material; this is a result of the attraction between particulate organic material (having a net negative ionic charge in seawater) and many cationic trace elements (possessing a net positive charge). In a marine aquarium, there are two main paths that the particulate organic material typically follows: it may be removed via filtration, such as through the use of activated carbon, protein skimming, and mechanical filters, or it

▲ ***With all the precision many tests and meters are able to provide, it is a bit frustrating that managing trace element levels is basically guesswork, but aquarists typically develop a regimen of supplementation that works for them.***

may be consumed by detrivores[2] and recycled back into the system. Trace elements becoming adsorbed to particulate organic material that becomes buried deep in the aquarium substrate may be temporarily liberated during sulfide reduction.

Biofilms[3], which typically form on inorganic substrates (such as live rock and live sand, in the context of marine aquaria), also adsorb trace elements and are a potential sink in aquatic environments.

Most synthetic salt blends do not disclose the concentration of trace elements, and as previously mentioned there are no feasible means of testing for the presence (much less the actual concentration) of trace elements available to hobbyists at this time. This creates a situation in which hobbyists must, in

[2] Detrivores are organisms which obtain most of their nutrients from feeding on the detritus present in an ecosystem.

[3] A biofilm may constitute the layer or layers of microbes, such as bacteria and cyanobacteria, that colonize a particulate substrate. The resulting film may be comprised of a myriad of organisms.

essence, blindly supplement aquaria with a trace element solution without really knowing what they're doing. It is therefore prudent to begin by dosing half the manufacturer's recommended dosage for the first few weeks of product use; then, so long as there are no problems evident, increase the dosage gradually up to full strength over the following weeks. Starting out at a lower dosage will not cause any harm to the livestock, and enables the hobbyist to notice subtle changes in the appearance of the system over time; it is these changes in appearance that the hobbyist must use to gauge when and to what extent trace element supplementation is required.

Many less obvious routes through which these elements are able to enter an aquarium exist. Tap water in some areas of the country contains minute amounts of heavy metals, which is one of the reasons to purify this water prior to adding it to an aquarium—let alone before drinking it! Some artificial salt mixes contain relatively high concentrations of heavy metals, another reason to research the salt you intend to use *before* purchasing that brand. These points are yet more reason to purify tap water and use a premium synthetic salt blend in aquaria.

At this point, perhaps a few words on the subject of supplement overdosing are warranted. Product overdose has been flogged by many hobbyists for years; this applies largely to those supplements which are of an inorganic nature, and could include the "chloride imbalance" dispute or the claim that trace elements in any concentrations are deadly to aquarium inhabitants. The first question that should be raised when this subject is addressed is what an overdose of one element or another would appear as. The argument, while credible in theory, is sometimes very difficult to substantiate in terms of actual experience. Hobbyists concerned about adding a product to an aquarium or who have questions regarding its use are encouraged to contact the manufacturer directly or speak with knowledgeable aquarium

This colony of Actinodiscus *grew from two individuals within the span of eight months. Such growth requires major, minor, and trace elements in the correct amounts. Unfortunately, many factors in a typical reef tank conspire to make trace elements unavailable to the livestock.* ▶

hobbyists that have some *direct experience* (not hearsay) with the product. At that point, comparisons between the hobbyists' aquaria and their experiences with specific products may be assessed and a decision made.

The rapid manner in which trace elements can become bound to organic material creates three potential routes for trace element depletion from a marine aquarium: protein skimming, activated carbon, and organic adsorption resins. Each of these filtration methods strips organic material from aquarium water, passively removing bound trace elements in the process. In addition, activated carbon may directly remove trace elements from water by trapping them in pores, including those that have been partially blocked by large organic molecules but allow passage for smaller substances to pass around the outsides. Cation-adsorption resins

and resin-impregnated filter pads, such as those employed to remove copper from water following medication, will also rapidly remove trace elements from water. Regular trace element supplementation is essential in those aquaria employing one or more of these filtration methods.

It is possible that the variation in coloration of cyanobacteria is due in part to the presence of certain trace elements and the colors these elements impart to their tissues. This may have some relevance to the age-old opinion that trace elements encourage the growth of cyanobacteria. Trace elements are often biolimiting, so claims that their presence is wholly responsible for a proliferation of cyanobacteria are plainly erroneous; cyanobacteria require adequate concentrations of latent organic matter in the environment in order to grow. In aquaria with inadequate filtration, organic matter accumulates and is generally present in a sufficient concentration for cyanobacterial growth. An aquarium may exist in this state without the obvious presence of cyanobacteria, however, until a hobbyist begins dosing a supplement containing some element that happens to be biolimiting in that particular aquarium; the growth of the cyanobacteria colonies in the aquarium will be approximately regulated by the abundance of the most biolimiting element being added.

◀ ***Protein skimmers, though extremely useful in removing substances before they can break down or decompose, can also remove trace elements. Activated carbon can also remove trace elements. Either of these filtration methods probably indicates a need for trace element supplementation.***

Confronted with such a problem, a hobbyist may turn to some chemical means of eliminating the cyanobacteria in the aquarium. This is inadvisable, and unnecessary. The addition of chemicals to an aquarium to combat the presence of some organism perceived as a nuisance can negatively impact other inhabitants in imperceptible ways, and can also cause numerous chemical processes to take place. The decomposition of cyanobacteria cells leads to the re-release of dissolved and particulate organic matter as well as that of trace elements that have accumulated in these tissues, providing nutrients for additional cyanobacterial as well as algal growth. It is likely that the majority of these trace elements will remain bound to organic matter, while those that are in aqueous form will become oxidized or form ion pairs; in any case, this collective process essentially represents a waste of trace elements and makes their management in desirable concentrations virtually impossible.

Non-conservative trace elements are very important to many biological reactions; therefore, they should be present in the aquarium at all times in the proper concentrations. The key to avoiding the issue outlined above is simply to utilize adequate means of organic material removal from an aquarium at all times and not allow it to accumulate. Should cyanobacteria suddenly become abundant in an aquarium, determine the source of the additional latent organic matter being utilized and eliminate it from the system (either by changing routines, eliminating certain types of foods that have been recently used, adsorption of organic matter by activated carbon or macroporous resins, or water changes), then physically siphon as much of the cyanobacteria as possible from the aquarium every day until their presence is made far less obvious. This is the most effective and safest means of ridding an aquarium of cyanobacteria.

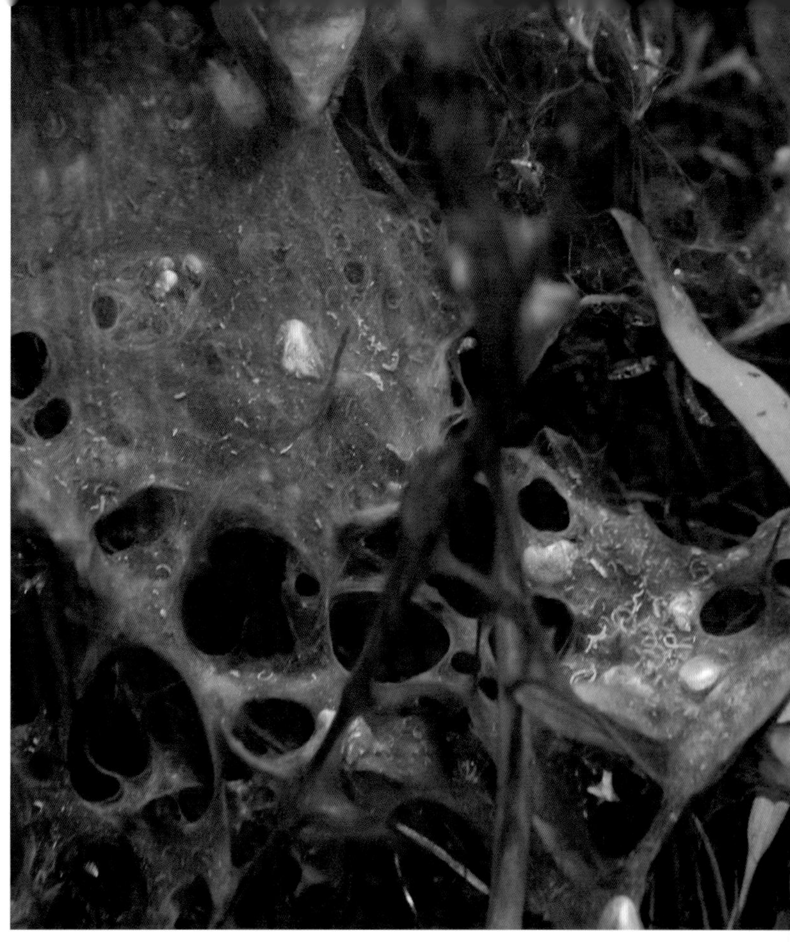

▲ *Cyanobacteria slime*
Although a cyanobacteria outbreak can follow dosing with trace elements, it is the overload of organic matter in the aquarium which is to blame; eliminate that and the cyanobacteria will decline despite the presence of adequate levels of trace elements.

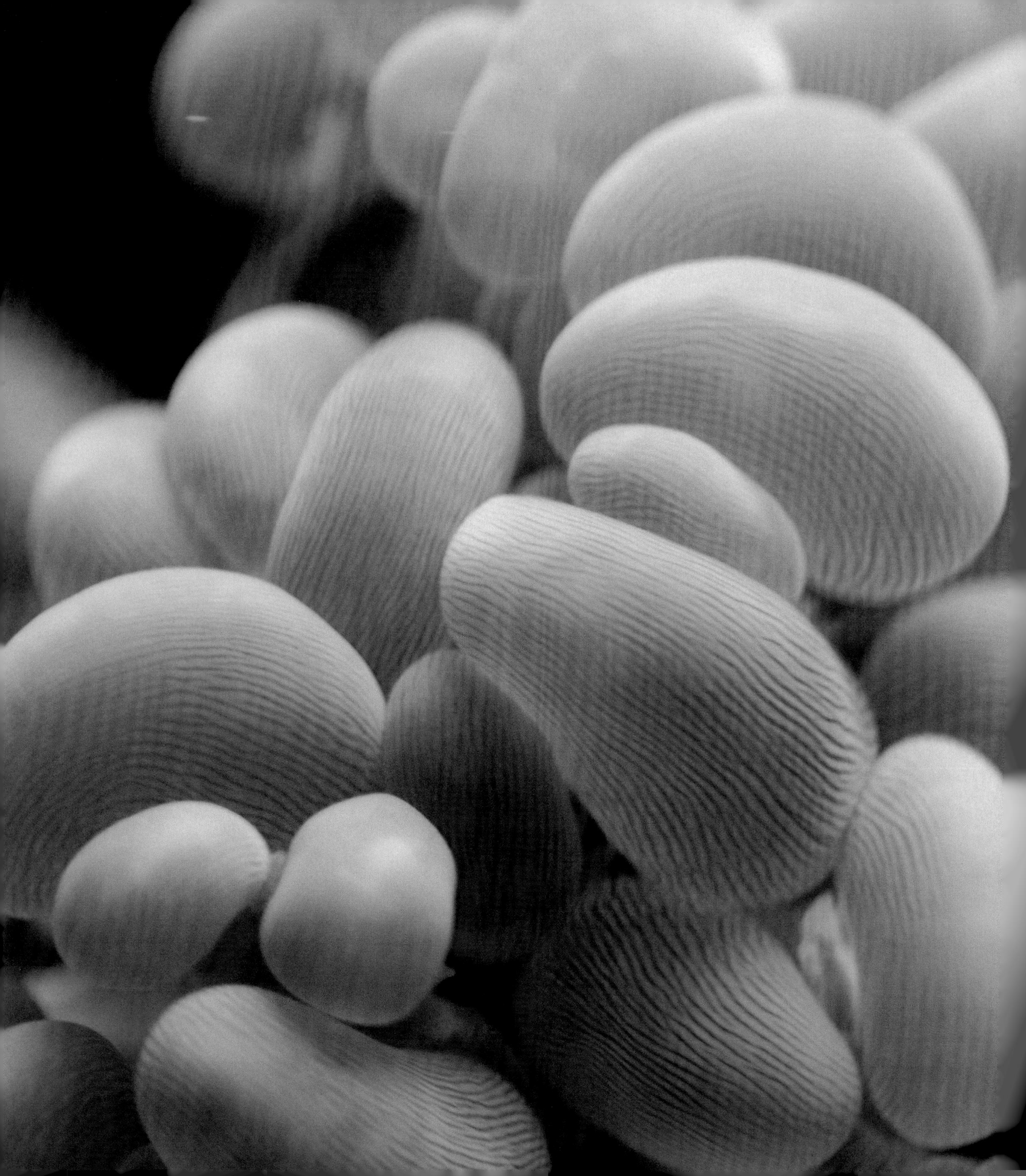

CHAPTER 18

Copper

Copper is one of the trace elements whose presence in marine aquaria has been much maligned; this is largely a result of the reputation that copper-based medications have for their toxicity to invertebrates. The irony is that copper is an essential element and exhibits nutrient-type behavior, indicating its importance to marine organisms. Hobbyists unaware of this fact often react radically toward manufacturers of trace element supplements that include copper among the list of elements provided, only to discover that they have gotten their facts wrong. Copper concentrations in trace element supplements are likely to be over one hundred times lower than they are in copper-based medications. Used as directed, these supplements pose no threat to livestock. While exceeding the maximum safe copper concentration can be disastrous in any marine aquarium, it is extremely unlikely that the amount of copper that will be dosed by a trace element supplement will approach a level of potential toxicity, even if severely overdosed.

Biomagnification and Bioaccumulation

It is prudent to expand now on the discussion of heavy metal biomagnification and bioaccumulation. Many marine invertebrates are composed of a high percentage of water, and constantly ingest and flush it out of their bodies. They may also consume organic

▲ *While angelfishes such as this potter's angelfish,* **Centropyge potteri**, *can withstand exposure to therapeutic concentrations of copper as a means of controlling ectoparasites, marine invertebrates cannot tolerate such elevated copper concentrations and will quickly die under such conditions.*

material and/or other invertebrates that contain relatively high amounts of heavy metals. These attributes put marine invertebrates at a relatively high risk of being poisoned by heavy metal accumulation; if these organisms are constantly exposed to elevated concentrations of these elements, it is far more likely that the concentration of heavy metal in their tissues will approach and possibly exceed the threshold for maintaining biological functioning. The key is simply to understand the process and use products containing essential elements in a sensible fashion. This philosophy applies to every aspect of aquarium care imaginable.

Copper Overdosing and Removal

Copper is useful for treating external parasites on fishes and should be administered in a quarantine aquarium. Overdosing a copper medication should be avoided at all costs, as it can completely kill the bed of nitrifying and denitrifying bacteria in a system; the decaying bacteria cause the oxygen concentration in the water to fall, which can cause fish to suffocate if not quickly remedied. This scenario can occur even within a quarantine aquarium, requiring the observation of fishes being medicated for several minutes or even hours after treatment has been administered. It is advisable to exercise due caution when using any copper medication. Methods of copper removal are the same as those outlined for the removal of trace elements in the previous chapter, however large-scale water changes with water containing no more than the natural seawater concentration of copper should be considered an additional and highly effective means of copper dilution.

By physically adding a copper medication to a reef aquarium at the manufacturer's recommended dosage, the hobbyist is assured that all invertebrates will react negatively, and probably die; this applies to medications containing organic (chelated) copper (i.e. methylated copper, copper EDTA and copper citrate) and/or ionic copper (such as that found in medications containing copper chloride or sulfate pentahydrate).

Converting Glass Tanks

Hobbyists wishing to convert a pre-existing marine fish-only glass aquarium that has been exposed to a copper-based medication to a reef system must be aware that copper is adsorbed into silicone sealant and gradually releases back into the system over time, creating a residual, albeit low, concentration of copper that may be deadly to invertebrates. A series of steps may be followed which will *generally* decrease the likelihood that this scenario occurs, but it's prudent to mention that a less expensive and safer long-term solution may simply be to purchase a new aquarium for the pending reef. Pre-owned glass aquaria that have never been exposed to copper-based medications are much safer when using them to house ornamental marine invertebrates. The following steps are provided only as a general guideline to use if purchasing such an aquarium isn't an option:

1. Remove the inhabitants from the existing aquarium and place them in a temporary system outfitted with support equipment necessary to maintain proper water parameters over a period of several weeks.

2. Purchase a new test kit capable of reading copper in marine aquaria.

3. With the seawater remaining in the aquarium and all filters and pumps operating as usual, drop the pH to around 6.0 using a pH-decreasing product. This will cause copper to be gradually released from the silicone caulk. Use a cation-adsorption resin or impregnated pad to adsorb all copper in solution.

4. Recharge the resin, if applicable, and place it back in the system; if using an impregnated pad, replace the exhausted pad with a new one.

5. Raise the pH back to 8.1 to 8.6

◀ *Hobbyists can avoid using copper supplements completely if they are dedicated to choosing the healthiest possible livestock, quarantining all new arrivals, providing these organisms with an appropriate diet, and maintaining the chemical and physical conditions in the aquarium to the requirements of these organisms.*

using a pH-increasing product, which should cause additional copper embedded in the silicone caulk to be released, making it removable by the resin or pad.

6. Repeat these steps until resins and pads no longer change color (indicating exhaustion) and no copper registers on the test kit.

Acrylic aquaria are chemically welded together and have no adhesives or surfaces for copper to penetrate. This is not solid grounds, however, to immediately consider acrylic aquaria that have been exposed to copper-based medications as completely safe

◀ *Crushed coral, sand, and live rock can leach acquired copper back into an aquarium, killing all invertebrates. When reusing such calcareous substances, it is important to test them for residual copper. If there is any doubt, find an alternative source.*

to house marine invertebrates. The same tests outlined above for glass aquaria should be followed for acrylic aquaria if for nothing more than peace of mind.

Copper in Calcareous Material

Calcareous substances—such as live rock and aragonite sand—that have been exposed to copper-based medications should not be used in reef aquaria due to the propensity for calcareous materials to absorb and then release copper into the system. To determine whether or not these media will leach copper into the aquarium, take some freshly made seawater and test it for ionic copper (the concentration should be too minute to measure), then place a piece of rock in the water and allow it to sit overnight, or better yet for several days. Test the water for ionic copper again; if any copper is

present, none of the rock should be placed into a reef aquarium. The same test can be performed on live sand. A far more effective means of performing this test is to submerge a sacrificial piece of rock in purified water, rather than seawater, for several days; doing so will aggressively cause absorbed ions to release into the water following the concentration gradient and will provide more reliable test results.

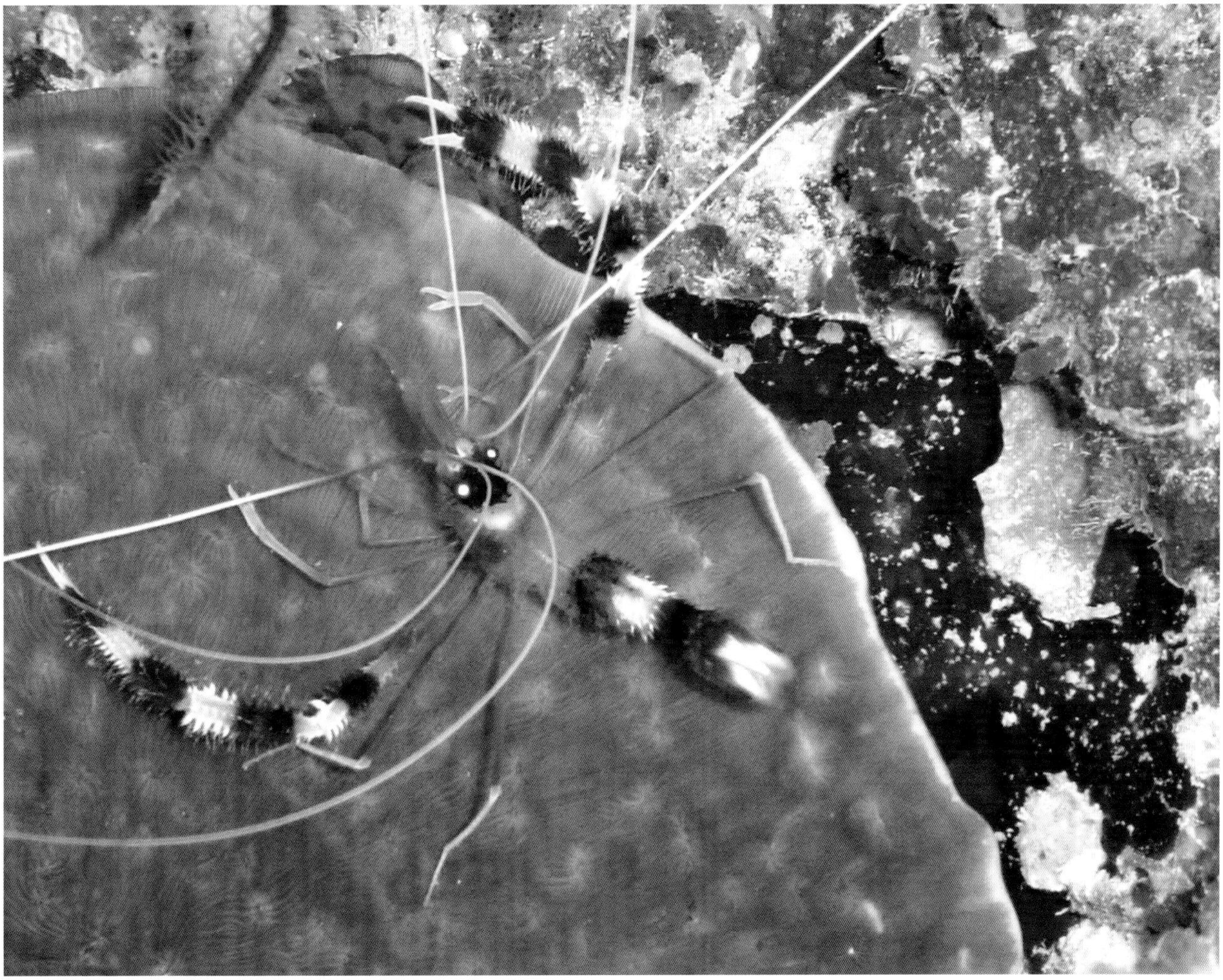

CHAPTER 19

Test Kits

The importance of maintaining water parameters within the livestock's tolerable ranges was mentioned in Chapter 1. While an experienced hobbyist may be able to make an educated guess regarding the relative quality of the water by observing the appearance of the livestock, the only way to know exactly what parameters are within or out of range is to test the water with a set of accurate test kits. Hobbyists with limited experience should test their aquarium water at least once a week in an attempt to familiarize themselves with changes in the appearance of aquarium inhabitants related to specific changes in water chemistry; until a hobbyist has a credible understanding of *why* some fish or invertebrate appears to be under stress, they are playing a guessing game with the lives of their aquarium inhabitants.

It is unfortunate and irrational that many hobbyists do not follow this advice. Considering the major investment in time and money that all types of marine aquaria require, it makes little sense why so many hobbyists are remiss to spend $50 on a complete array of test kits. One coral alone may cost well over $100, while many commonly available fish species cost even more than that. Granted, a relatively small percentage of marine aquarium hobbyists may ever own a single fish or coral that cost over $100, but chances are that the sum of their livestock purchases will be well in excess of this amount.

Is the additional money required to buy test kits such a big deal? Stated a different way, is it wise to risk the health and lives of these animals because of an aversion to purchasing an accurate ammonia test kit for less than $15? There really is no excuse for not owning a set of accurate test kits *and using them* on a regular basis.

Figure 19.1 illustrates important tests to be performed in different types of aquaria.

Figure 19.1. Recommended Water Analysis for Marine Aquaria

Parameter	System Type	Testing Frequency
Salinity	All Marine Aquaria	Weekly
pH	All Marine Aquaria	Weekly
Alkalinity	All Marine Aquaria	Weekly
Ammonia	All Marine Aquaria	Weekly
Nitrite/Nitrate	All Marine Aquaria	Weekly
Calcium	Reef Aquaria	Weekly
Magnesium	Reef Aquaria	Weekly
Iodine	Reef Aquaria	Weekly
Strontium	Reef Aquaria	Weekly
Phosphate	Reef Aquaria	As conditions dictate
Silicate	Reef Aquaria	As conditions dictate
Iron	Reef Aquaria	As conditions dictate
Copper	Fish-Only Aquaria	As conditions dictate
Dissolved Oxygen	All Marine Aquaria	As conditions dictate
Dissolved Carbon Dioxide	All Marine Aquaria	As conditions dictate

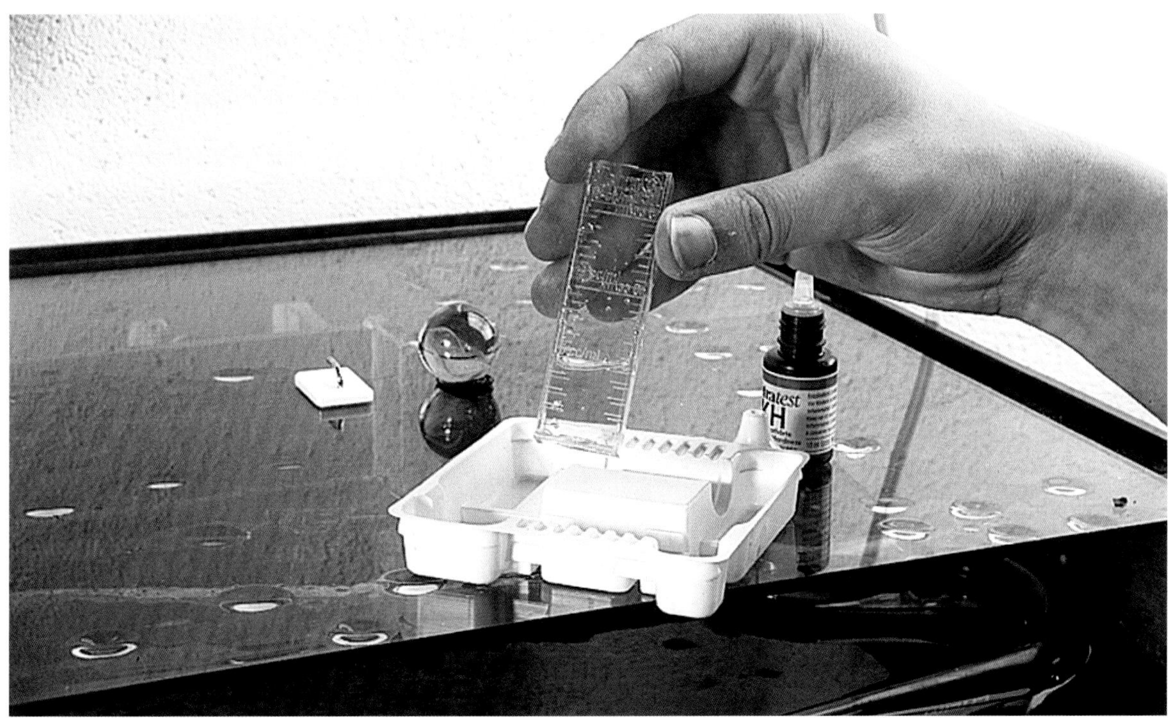

▲ *Test kits come in a wide range of qualities and prices. Don't skimp, or you'll likely get inferior results, which can lead to poor water quality and sick fish.*

Reliability and Accuracy

Test kit reliability and accuracy are of paramount importance; purchasing inaccurate test kits is a complete waste of money. Marine aquarium hobbyists are accustomed to paying premium prices to obtain the best products available for aquarium care, largely due to the fact that quality ingredients are expensive. Test kits are no exception—although a test kit doesn't have to be expensive to be accurate, experience has shown that the cheapest kits on the market are invariably the least accurate ones, and therefore are far less likely to provide reliable readings. Inexpensive test kits are absolutely no bargain, for the kit will eventually require replacement with a more accurate (and likely more expensive) one; the cost of replacing any livestock that perished as a result of trusting false readings should also be considered.

Inaccuracy

Test kits marketed by companies selling everything from fish food to pond filters seem to produce the least accurate results when compared to laboratory-grade test kits. The most accurate aquarium-use test kits are manufactured or marketed by companies that deal specifically with water chemistry with regards to the majority of their remaining product line. These companies have better quality control over their product and understand the reactions taking place in the respective kits, and therefore can provide a better product and customer service to inquiring hobbyists.

Choosing a Test Kit

The very first thing that hobbyists should look for on the outside of a test kit package is an expiration date. The accuracy of reagents gradually decreases with time; typically, they have a useful shelf life of approximately one year from the date of manufacture. The expiration date is an indication of how viable the test results are likely to be at the date of purchase. In general, replacing reagents annually is recommended. Finding extremely unusual water parameters but having aquarium inhabitants that appear completely healthy and normal is often an indication that test kit reagents require replacement.

To maximize the effective shelf life of reagents, all test kits should be stored in a cool environment, out of direct sunlight or aquarium lighting.

Colorimetric vs. Titrimetric

Most test kits available to aquarium hobbyists are either colorimetric or titrimetric. Colorimetric kits rely on a reaction to create a shade within a color range; the shade is then compared with a color chip or scale, thereby providing a reading. Hobbyists familiar with these types of test kits know that it can be quite difficult to determine the exact

▲ *A colony of Pacific mushroom polyps,* Ricordia yuma, *may fetch $100 in many aquarium stores. But they are not very durable relative to similar invertebrates commonly encountered in the hobby, and especially need expertly maintained water quality.*

reading; this is a result of having to compare colors between the sample and the progressive color scale provided by the manufacturer. This difficulty may be no fault of the manufacturer, but rather is often due to the fact that each specific color corresponds with a specific value. Polling other hobbyists or family members present at the time of performing a hard-to-read test can produce a consensus that is better than not having a decisive answer. Test kits featuring colored paper scales are less desirable than those

that rely upon colored plastic chips or discs to provide a numerical value, as colored paper often fades unless treated for exposure to heat, water, and ultraviolet light.

With titrimetric test kits, a standard solution, or titrant, is added to a sample (aquarium water, for our purposes) containing an unknown amount of some substance. A dramatic change in the color of the sample indicates that the titrant added has reacted with all of the substance present in that sample; in other words, the reaction is complete. The volume of titrant required to complete the reaction is then used to calculate the amount of the target substance present within that sample. Generally, titrimetric kits are easier to read than colorimetric kits.

Not all parameters are offered in both titrimetric and colorimetric test kits; rather, one or the other is usually available. Phosphate, silicate, ammonia, nitrite, nitrate, pH, iodine, copper, and iron are typically tested with colorimetric kits, while alkalinity, calcium, magnesium, and strontium are tested with titrimetric kits.

Testing Parameters

The recommended ranges of parameters in Figure 1.1 may be referred to when deciding which test kits best suit the hobbyist's particular needs. In general, any test kit sold for

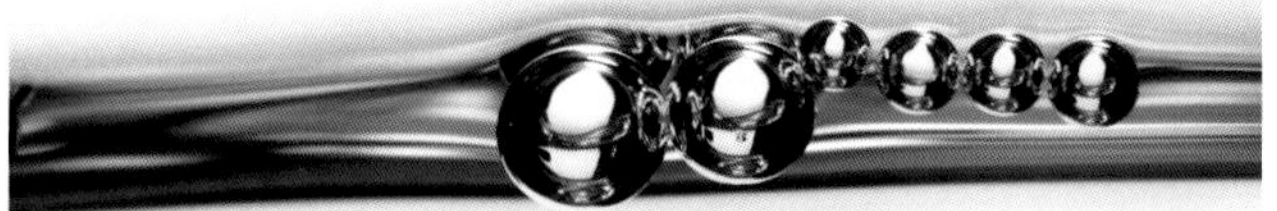

A Good Investment

When one considers the enjoyment to be had from many aspects of the marine aquarium hobby and the considerable time and money invested in setting up an aquarium, it makes no sense to not purchase a set of high-accuracy test kits to help maintain the system. Most problems encountered by hobbyists are the result of not regularly testing their water, and therefore not knowing what is really going on in their aquaria. One hundred dollars spent on test kits to maintain an aquarium that cost thousands of dollars to set up and stock represents the hobbyist's insurance that many chemistry-related mistakes can be avoided.

use in a marine aquarium should be able to read within the desired ranges for respective parameters; the usefulness of a kit relies on its measurable range and accuracy. For example, it does no good to purchase a test kit for phosphate that cannot read concentrations between 0 and 1.0 ppm when the target concentration is below 0.05 ppm.

Regular testing of aquarium water is the only way to gain an understanding of the relationship between water parameters and the associated changes in the appearance of the tank's inhabitants. By understanding how to interpret results, hobbyists will certainly increase their success rate with marine aquaria.

Water Quality

A wide range of topics have been covered in Part 1 of this book. Remember that before filtration, lighting, and all else, the chemical characteristics of the aquarium water play the biggest role in determining the success of an aquarium hobbyist. It is to this specific topic that beginning hobbyists should pay the most detail, because as they will discover, it doesn't matter how much time and money are invested into an aquarium setup if the water quality doesn't meet the needs of the inhabitants.

Part Two

Water Purification

CHAPTER 20

The Need to Purify Tap Water

At the present time, tap water in many locales contains numerous materials toxic to humans and aquatic life; this raises the question of whether this water is even safe for human consumption, much less use in an aquarium. Heavy metals, pesticides, herbicides, industrial pollutants (carbon tetrachloride, vinyl chloride, benzene etc.), petroleum products, chlorine, radium, and radon gas are some of the more notable substances often present in tap water supplies, both municipal and private. Of particular interest to aquarium hobbyists, phosphates and silicates present in municipal water cause rapid growth of undesirable algae, cyanobacteria, and diatoms. Addressing the two major substances (or contaminants, by definition) in municipal water (and often in well water), chlorine and chloramines, provides the basis for advocating water purification.

Chlorine and Chloramine

To keep the concentrations of pathogens in municipal water supplies under control, treatment facilities typically utilize chlorine and chloramines as biocides. The negative impact that these substances can have on aquatic life is significant and requires that tap water be properly treated before being added to an aquarium. Chlorine and chloramines are oxidants that enter living cells and inhibit metabolism, effectively causing the demise of the organism. Fishes exposed to low concentrations of chlorine and chloramines typically

*Many species of marine fish, such as this lyretail anthias (*Pseudanthias squamipinnis*), fare much better in saltwater that has been prepared with purified source water rather that that which is made from straight "tap water" and a synthetic salt mix. The chemical characteristics of tap water differ greatly by region, sometimes even within the same town, and seasonal changes in the concentration of substances present in tap water may dramatically impact the health of marine aquarium inhabitants.*

suffer from anoxia (lack of oxygen) in their bloodstreams as a result of the interaction of these substances with hemoglobin, and appear to gasp at the water's surface. The maximum tolerable concentration of chlorine (in any form) varies from species to species, so the maximum concentration allowed in an aquarium should be below that of the most sensitive species present. Toxicology studies suggest that 0.002 mg/L chlorine is the maximum concentration at which no observable effects are seen in aquatic organisms (including invertebrates). This indicates that at concentrations greater than 0.002 mg/L chlorine, aquatic organisms begin to show signs of toxicity. Beneficial bacteria and other microorganisms in an aquarium are quickly killed by exposure to these substances. Taking these points into perspective leads one to the inevitable conclusion that total eradication of chlorine and chloramines from tap water provides the greatest degree of safety for aquarium husbandry.

Chlorine

Chlorine is administered as a gas, and the concentration of chlorine in the water supply can change on a seasonal basis as a result of water temperature or environmental concerns. Chlorine is highly reactive, and although it acts much more quickly against microorganisms than chloramines do, it also has the major drawback of forming trihalomethanes (which are suspected carcinogens) via interaction with organic substances. Chlorine gas also escapes from water rapidly. This poses a problem for water treatment facilities: the farther the water must travel from the facility, the longer the chlorine has to react with organic material and the more time it has to escape from water. These aspects of chlorine have ultimately led to the use of additional or alternative means of water disinfection, namely the use of chloramines.

Dangers of Chlorine

Chlorine is one of the halide elements, and is somewhat similar to iodine in terms of oxidation potential. It readily oxidizes organic matter, making it well suited for use in a swimming pool or in sanitizing tap water, but it isn't healthy to ingest in large quantities. It doesn't take much chlorine gas to cause respiratory problems, and it's lethal at relatively low concentrations.

Chloramines

Chloramines are compounds formed by combining chlorine gas with liquefied ammonia gas in water. The result is a molecule with low molecular weight that stays in the water longer and is a relatively effective biocide. There are three forms that chloramines may take, depending on the chemical characteristics of the water in which they are formed: monochloramine, dichloramine, and trichloramine. The difference among these forms is essentially the number of chloride ions possessed—monochloramine bears one chloride ion, dichloramine

A plethora of colonial polyps, some having colonized a beer bottle in a reef aquarium. Such a display is not easily created using unfiltered tap water and a low-quality synthetic salt mix, as impurities and contaminants are utilized in conjunction with intense light by such "nuisance" organisms as cyanobacteria and various types of microalgae, both of which detract from the appearance of a marine aquarium and may pose some threat to the inhabitants themselves (particularly to sessile invertebrates).

bears two, and trichloramine bears three. (A fourth species of chloramine is organic chloramine, but it has negligible biocidal capacity and is not included in the remainder of this discussion.)

The predominant form of chloramine utilized in drinking water is monochloramine. It is a better biocide than the other two forms of chloramines and is stable at a pH greater than roughly 7.5; lower pH values and higher chlorine concentrations yield dichloramine and/or trichloramine. In order to keep the presence of these less desirable forms of chloramines at a minimum and maximize the percentage of monochloramine present, the pH of municipal drinking water is usually buffered to range between 7.5 and 9. (Slightly basic pH also inhibits corrosion of pipes, another reason to maintain a pH greater than 7.)

In contrast to chlorine, chloramines form few to no trihalomethanes. However, because chloramines are relatively ineffective against certain microorganisms (viruses in particular), municipalities nearly always combine chloramines and chlorine for more complete pathogenic eradication. The ratio of chloramines to chlorine used in any given area is largely a factor of the amount of organic material in the water supply; the more organic matter present, the greater the potential formation of trihalomethanes, and so the higher the ratio of chloramines to chlorine must become. This fact and the perceived need for water disinfection by the municipality dictate that chemical characteristics of drinking water all over the country may be slightly different from one another.

▲ *To obtain water suitable for growing coral frags into colonies it is almost always necessary to purify the tap water used to mix artificial seawater.*

Tap Water Concentrations

Regardless of the ratio employed, the Environmental Protection Agency (EPA) has declared that the maximum allowable residual concentration of chlorine (denoting a combination of different forms of chlorine) in drinking water supplies be 4 mg/L. A poll of several cities around the United States revealed that some cities maintain the total chlorine concentration within a range of 2 to 3 mg/L, while the majority seem to be in the 3 to 4 mg/L range. Chloramine concentrations in water supplies tend to range between 1.0 and 2.5 mg/L, which means that the overall contribution of chlorine from these chloramines is approximately 0.69 to 1.72 mg/L, corresponding to an ammonia concentration of 0.31 to 0.78 mg/L. At the time of this writing, no

▲ *The chemicals used in sterilizing tap water in the United States require treatment of the water to render it safe for aquarium use. The fact that many municipal water companies vary the way in which they treat the water only complicates matters more for the aquarist.*

U.S. cities appear to be treating their water with only chloramines rather than a combination of chloramines and chlorine.

Water Treatment

The use of chloramines poses one major problem to municipalities, which is corrosion of lead and copper pipes, releasing elevated concentrations of lead and copper ions into the water; this is a direct result of the presence of ammonia in the water once the chloramines have reacted with the pathogens they are meant to destroy. To help combat this corrosion issue (and help decrease the concentrations of these potentially harmful elements in the water), municipalities may add orthophosphate and silicates as a protective measure. Additionally, a percentage of the free ammonia may be converted into nitrite and nitrate by nitrifiers in the water. So in summary, the water is likely to contain nitrite, nitrate, iron, copper, silicates, and phosphate, as well as the chlorine and ammonia present.

Just as with other gases, the solubility of chlorine gas is a function of the water's temperature. Cold water holds more gas in solution than warmer water, hence the old practice of "aging" cold tap water in a bucket overnight to allow the chlorine to escape and make it safer for use in an aquarium, which works even today. Even with heavy aeration from a pump, allowing water to sit in a bucket overnight will not significantly rid it of chloramines, however. For hobbyists not 100% certain that their tap water is treated only with chlorine, and that their water company *never* obtains water from chloraminated sources, this overnight degassing is unreliable. Chloramines are odorless and tasteless, further compounding the problem of determining whether the water is safe without first neutralizing chlorine and then performing a test for ammonia.

Neutralization

Utilizing some means of neutralizing the chlorine and chloramines in tap water is essential. There are three main methods employed to achieve this goal: treatment of the water with a chemical that changes the form of the offending substances and makes them harmless, adsorption with activated carbon, or removal via reverse osmosis or ion exchange (deionization). Limitations on budget, time, and understanding of these methods by hobbyists largely dictate the method they choose to employ. Formal purification, rather than merely treating it for one or two unwanted substances, is the most effective means of preparing water for use in an aquarium.

CHAPTER 21

Principles of Water Purification

For the remainder of Part 2, the term "water purification" will appear frequently. The EPA has standards on what they consider "purification" to be, but which are far too limiting and wordy; for the purposes of aquarium husbandry, their definition has been modified to: *the filtration of water by passing it through some medium such as a sediment prefilter, activated carbon, reverse osmosis membrane, or deionization resins, treating it with ozone, or processing it with distillation.*

Great strides have been made in the past few decades to filter water thoroughly of the contaminants commonly found in it. Technology that was developed to prepare water for use in laboratories and for drinking was applied to the aquarium hobby by aquarists seeking to have the greatest possible control over water chemistry. By beginning with water that may be over 99.9% free of contaminants, the hobbyist has a basis for providing a chemical environment in which all constituents in solution are known to within a very small margin of error (provided that they use products listing a guaranteed analysis).

Two Types of Purification

When starting out with water from the tap, there are essentially two forms of water purification utilized in the aquarium hobby: reverse osmosis and deionization. Distillation and ozonation (excluding its use in an aquarium for increasing ORP) are more commonly used in operations preparing raw water for bottling.

Bottled Water

Bottled water available in grocery stores is often of questionable quality, and is always relatively expensive. This water is made for human consumption, not expressly for use in marine aquaria, and the purification process this water goes through may include distillation in copper tubing. Due to the astringent nature of purified water, a potential exists for toxic concentrations of copper to be released from the tubing, winding up in the finished product; the previous chapter illustrated the reasons as to why this is undesirable. The best way to determine whether or not bottled water is of high-enough quality and is free of copper and other heavy metals is to have it professionally tested; alternately, a measurement of the TDS present in the water provides a general estimate of the actual purity.

Aquarium-Store Water

For hobbyists currently using store-bought water in marine aquaria and who want to switch to water purified via reverse osmosis and/or deionization but are not prepared to make the investment in a water purification system, many aquarium stores sell purified water as a service to their customers. The drawback is that the expense of purchasing this water quickly adds up to the cost of a filtration system. A gallon of water at the grocery store costs about 50 cents, a gallon of purified water at an

◀ *Zoanthids such as those shown here provide tremendous diversity of color to a marine aquarium, are relatively inexpensive as invertebrates go, and have relatively modest chemical and lighting demands. Though they can tolerate sub-optimal conditions for varying lengths of time, lighting of medium to high intensity and water chemistry that closely mirrors that of natural seawater will encourage their proliferation and colonization of bare surfaces in an aquarium; purifying tap water used to make synthetic saltwater is the basis of the latter point.*

aquarium shop may cost 25 cents, but a gallon of water purified with a home unit can cost less than one cent! It's not difficult to see how fast one of these units can pay for itself. Many hobbyists use tap water treated with a chlorine or chloramine neutralizer and nothing else, but by and large most of the truly spectacular marine aquarium displays in homes, offices, hotels, restaurants, casinos, etc., are maintained with water that has been purified with reverse osmosis and/or deionization. In this case a picture is certainly worth a thousand words.

Purification systems

Hobbyists shopping for a water purification system may be justifiably confused about the available features and which unit may best suit their needs. The first step is to obtain the TDS reading of the cold tap water, as well as the water pressure from the line that will feed the unit. Second, request a water analysis from the

▲ *Longnose Hawkfish* (Oxycirrhites typus) *on the prowl for small invertebrates and fishes. The diversity of colors and shapes among reef fishes is spectacular.*

municipal water supplier (these are free), and be sure to ask what the average concentration of chlorine in the water is from season to season. Hobbyists on city water are finding more frequently that their town buys water from different locations at different times; while one town may treat its water with chlorine, another might treat with chloramines. Acting on this information can help prolong the life of the reverse osmosis membrane. Only after performing an accurate analysis on the source water can one say with some certainty that the use of a particular water filtration unit will be more advantageous than another.

The second important factor that will influence your decision should be the number of gallons of purified water required on a daily basis. Units are rated at the maximum number of gallons they can produce each day (gallons per day or gpd) *under optimal conditions*. Because it's very rare for tap water to meet all of the criteria at the same time, the amount of purified water produced daily by a reverse osmosis or deionization filter typically is less than the manufacturer's maximum rating. This is simply due to the variability in characteristics of tap water from location to location. Although there are ways to optimize performance, hobbyists who absolutely need to produce 25 gallons of purified water each day are well advised to purchase a unit rated to purify more than that.

The following are the "optimal conditions" mentioned a moment ago:

- Water pressure of at least 80 psi
- Water temperature of 75°F (24°C)
- TDS of less than 250 ppm

If the source water meets these criteria, a purification unit *should* produce at least as much water as the manufacturer claims. If it doesn't, check the unit's instructions and make sure that it's assembled properly; there may be a fitting in the wrong location or the membrane may not be properly seated in the housing (if applicable).

Typically, reverse osmosis units have better production volume during warm months, as the water temperature in most locales is within the optimal range; during the winter and early spring, production decreases dramatically. To combat this problem,

These stony coral frags can truly be called domesticated. They are clones of corals that have been widely shared among North American aquarists. To a considerable extent, the availability of reliable water purification has made such things—which could hardly be imagined a few decades ago—possible.

Invertebrates are the basis of the reef hobby, and to keep these delicate animals, the quality of the water used is as essential as the purity of the salt mix.

hobbyists are often tempted to mix hot and cold source water—*don't do it.* Only cold water should be used in reverse osmosis and deionization systems, as hot water typically has a high concentration of dissolved metals present from having passed through the water heater; these metals will impact the membrane and prematurely exhaust the cation exchange resin in the deionization canister. Additionally, if the water temperature is not closely monitored and controlled, excessively hot water can destroy the glue that holds reverse osmosis membranes together, causing them to unravel in the membrane housing and rendering them completely ineffective. To warm source water safely, create a simple and inexpensive heat-exchange system:

1. Obtain 40 to 50 feet of the tubing that connects the water source to the purification unit input (typically a sediment pre-filter), and connect the unit to the source with this tube.

2. Coil the tubing into large loops and drop it in a bucket or garbage can filled with regular tap water, and into this bucket place one or more submersible aquarium heaters with adjustable thermostats.

3. Set the temperature on the heater(s) to the highest temperature possible and allow time for the water in the vessel to warm sufficiently.

4. Turn the source water on. As water moves through the coiled tubing, it will pick up heat from the warmer surrounding water.

5. Test the temperature of the water entering the purification unit and adjust the thermostat setting to heat the source water to the aforementioned 70° to 77°F; be aware that as the ground temperature rises and falls with changing weather the temperature of water inside the vessel will need to be adjusted in order to compensate.

Hobbyists with high-TDS source water (>200 ppm) are advised to contact manufacturers of reverse-osmosis and deionization filters *prior* to purchasing a unit. Discussing the chemical characteristics of the source water to be purified with the company's technical support personnel will provide insight into the performance that can be expected from a given filtration unit, as well as suggestions about how the hobbyist might optimize the unit for their specific situation.

CHAPTER 22

Reverse Osmosis Filtration

Reverse osmosis (RO), also known as hyper filtration (HF), is the process of forcing source water through a semi-permeable membrane (essentially a tightly wound sheet of material with very tiny perforations), removing dissolved and particulate substances that are physically larger than the diameter of the pores and/or are electrochemically rejected by the membrane material. These substances consist largely of high-molecular-weight components such as organic molecules, low-molecular-weight components such as monatomic and polyatomic ions, and microorganisms such as bacteria and viruses. Entrained gases, such as ammonia, are not rejected by reverse osmosis membranes and pass freely through and into the purified water (also known as permeate or filtrate), as a result of their ability to compress under the intense pressure inside the membrane housing (their neutral electrical charge may also play a role in their ability to pass through the membrane).

The pressure inside the housing is typically in the range of 40 to 70 psi, but operating pressures up to 200 psi may be utilized on high-capacity commercial units to increase both the removal rate and rate[1] of water purification. Few people have an understanding of what such enormous pressure is capable of; one way of illustrating it is that a pressure of 100 psi can launch a golf ball from a pneumatic cannon about 1,000

[1] The removal rate is the percentage of a substance that will be taken out of the source water by passing it through a purification process; the higher the filter's removal rate, the more pure the product water is. It stands to reason that purification units capable of the highest removal rates are also the most expensive.

▲ *Blue mandarinfish* (Synchiropus splendens) *browsing for microinvertebrates. Differences in the technologies applied in reverse osmosis and deionization make one method better for some hobbyists than the other; additionally, water temperature, chemistry, and the line pressure at the point of purification will greatly influence, and even determine, which method will be most effective. The method of water purification utilized is not as important as the quality of the final product.*

yards. It is for this reason that RO units under such pressure must be mounted securely and in such a manner that bystanders cannot stand directly at either end of the membrane housing. This way, in the unlikely event that the housing developed a crack and burst, no one would be seriously injured.

Spiral-Wound RO Membrane

Figure 22.1 shows two of the many layers that make up a spiral-wound RO membrane. Each layer is composed of permeate collection material sandwiched between membrane material; layers are separated by feed channel spacer material. These layers are wound around a center pipe possessing holes to channel the permeate into a single tube. A very thin layer of material coats the side of the membrane material that is exposed to the source water; this "skin layer" helps prevent the impaction of substances in the membrane itself and prolongs the effectiveness of the membrane. As the figure demonstrates, the membrane allows water (and little else) to pass through and into a layer of permeate collection material; the permeate then follows the spiraled collection material into the center pipe. The remaining water, known as the concentrate, contains water and the substances rejected by the membrane as a result of being physically larger than the membrane material pore size; the concentrate passes into a port that is offset from the center of the membrane housing, and then into a waste tube. This type of RO filtration is known as crossflow, referring to the parallel path that the concentrate follows with respect to the membrane material.

How They Work

Interestingly, there is no consensus on the exact mechanism by which RO membranes operate. There are two principal theories, presented here in a highly simplified fashion. One holds that the membrane material allows the passage of water and not only rejects substances larger than the pore sizes, but also those smaller than the pores and possessing an electrical charge (i.e. ions); the other theory suggests that RO membranes are simply porous films that allow the water to pass based on pressure inside the housing while substances in the water are rejected on the basis of concentration gradients. Regardless of the mechanism, the actual pore size of RO membrane material is so small that it is unable to be measured by even the most

Figure 22.1. Spiral-Wound RO Membrane

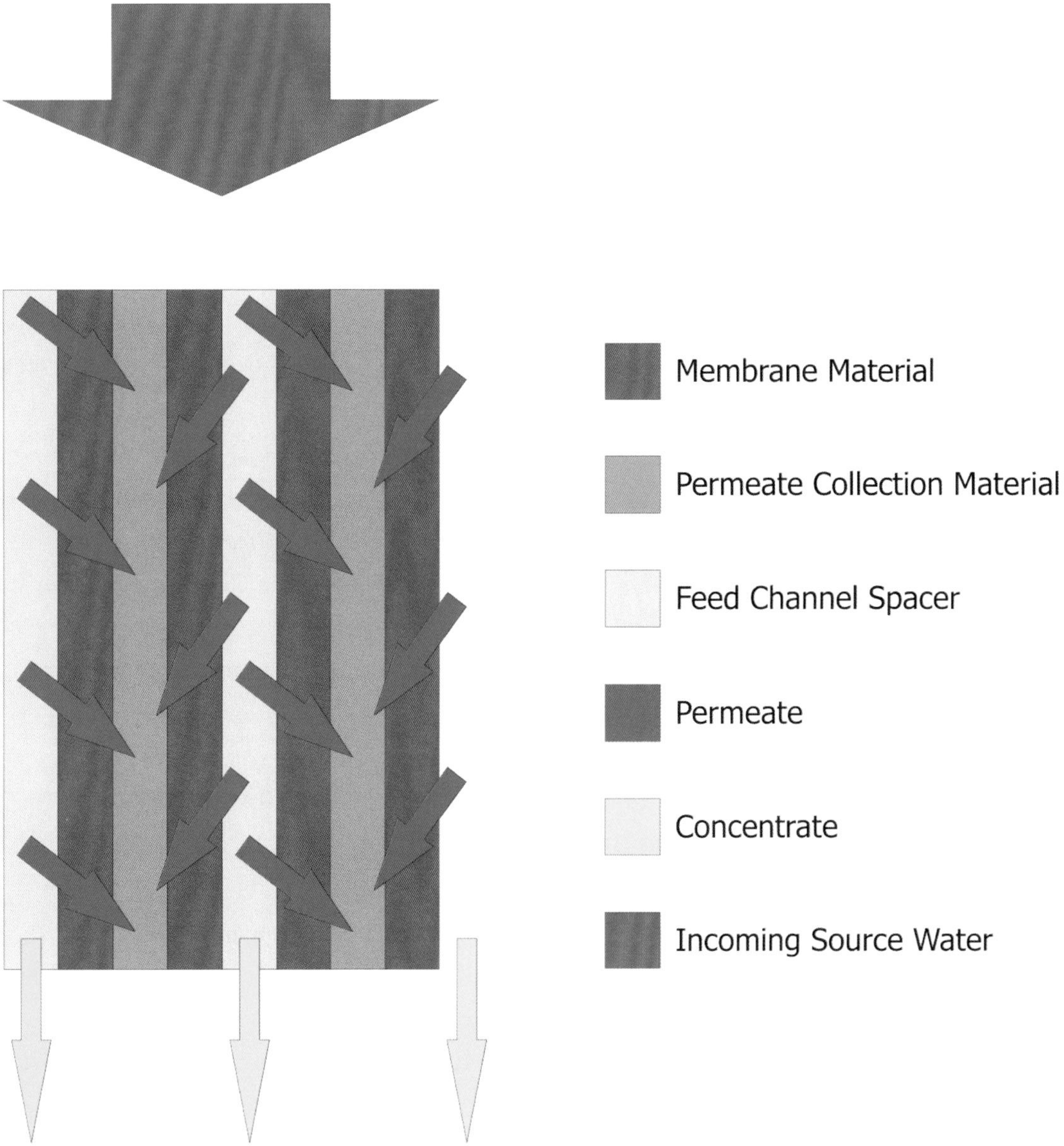

advanced microscopes. In order for a membrane to meet the criteria that qualify it as RO, however, the pore diameter must be no larger than 15 angstroms (Å) (1 angstrom = 1×10^{-10} meters, or 0.10 nanometers), with the smallest pore diameter likely to be in the realm of 5 Å. Considering the fact that most monatomic ions have a diameter of less than 4 Å (based on their known atomic radiuses), strong evidence exists to support the belief that charged substances are rejected by RO membranes on the basis of dielectric repulsion.

The purity of the permeate depends on the physical and chemical characteristics of the membrane material used, the tap water pressure, and the water temperature. Typical removal rates of 90 to 99.5% of most substances present may be expected from a well-maintained reverse osmosis unit. Under optimal conditions and if properly cared for, such a unit can produce up to 10,000 gallons of purified water at a cost of less than a penny per gallon.

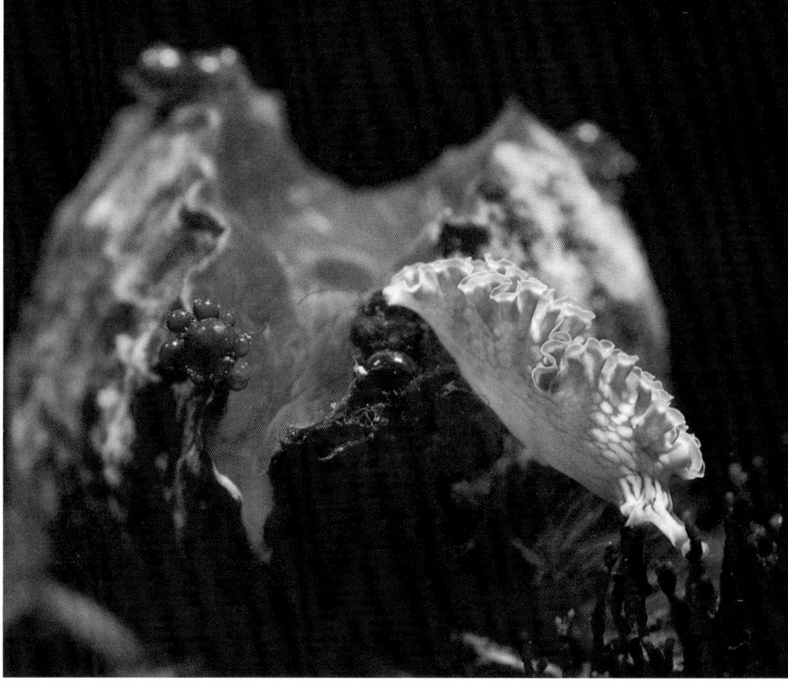

▲ *A lettuce slug* (Tridachia sp.) *on the move. Aquarium hobbyists are blessed to have such beautiful creatures available for housing in the enclosed aquatic environments they assemble and maintain, and to have the means of providing the pure water these animals need.*

Waste Water

The drawback to reverse osmosis filtration is that considerable water is wasted in the purification process. This "waste water" (the concentrate) contains the majority of the dissolved substances that were present in the source water. The substances that were not washed out in the waste water end up in one of two places: impacted in the pores (if substance size

< pore diameter), or in the purified water (if substance size < pore diameter). It is the impaction of these substances in the pores that slowly decreases the membrane's effectiveness, and ultimately requires that it be replaced. Back-flushing the membrane for a few minutes once a week helps dislodge some of the impacted substances and helps lengthen the life span of the membrane. High-efficiency reverse osmosis units waste approximately two to four gallons of water for every gallon of water that is purified; less efficient units may waste up to 10 gallons of water for each gallon purified. Hobbyists can contact the manufacturers of these units before making a purchase to find out the ratio of purified to waste water to expect.

Membranes

There are two main types of membranes used in reverse osmosis filtration: cellulose acetate (CA, most commonly cellulose triacetate, or CTA) and polyamide polymer (PP, most commonly thin film composite, or TFC or TFM).

Cellulose Acetate

CA membrane material is organic in nature (also known as "integral"), and is able to remove 88 to 94% of most impurities from source water. An average of 50 to 70% of the nitrate present in tap water can be removed by a CA membrane. Because the membrane is composed of a cellulose material, it is susceptible to decomposition by bacteria and other microbes present in source water, requiring that water directly entering the membrane be chlorinated or chloraminated. Purified water exiting the membrane is then diverted through an activated carbon filter to break down chloramines and remove chlorine. Because of the need for chlorinated source water, a CA membrane cannot be used on a well water system unless it is regularly chlorinated. In this respect, a CA membrane is generally able to withstand continuous exposure to up to 2.0 ppm total chlorine, whereas a membrane composed of composite materials typically cannot tolerate even 0.1 ppm of total chlorine.

▲ *An egg ribbon laid by lettuce slugs. The future of the aquarium hobby will be somewhat dependent upon the success rates that hobbyists have in captive reproduction of animals like lettuce slugs.*

CA membranes require far higher operating pressure than do PP membranes to work to optimal performance, a fact that should be taken into consideration by those hobbyists living in homes with low water pressure (for they will likely require a booster pump to increase line pressure when using a CA membrane). The main attraction of CA membranes for hobbyists is their relatively low cost when compared to PP membranes; they can be up to 60% less expensive than their composite membrane counterparts.

Polyamide Polymer

PP membranes are able to remove roughly 92 to 99% of most impurities

and 95% of the nitrate from source water, and they have better resistance to high water temperature (up to approximately 95°F) and pH extremes (pH values less than 3 and greater than 8) than does the CA material. A PP membrane is composed essentially of a plastic material which, as previously mentioned, is intolerant of chlorine and chloramines; therefore all water entering the membrane must first pass through an activated carbon filter. Regardless of the concentration of chlorine compounds in the tap water and the grade of carbon used, activated carbon filters will become exhausted and require replacement one or more times before the membrane is no longer effective. Manufacturers of RO units should have this information available for interested hobbyists, enabling the user to replace activated carbon when some volume of water has passed through the unit and thereby protecting the membrane from chlorine-induced damage.

Silica Removal

The removal of silica from source water is of great interest to reef aquarium hobbyists in particular. Both CA and PP membranes are capable of rejecting all of the colloidal silica present in source water, but PP membranes are more effective at removing ionic silica (PPs exhibit up to 99% ionic silica removal versus a 95% maximum removal rate for CAs).

Polyamide polymer membranes are recommended in areas in which water companies make heavy use of silicates. What a shame if your view of a beautiful soft coral such as this were marred by a diatom film on everything in the aquarium.

In areas of the country where the heavy use of water glass by municipal water companies contributes to massive diatom blooms in marine aquaria, the use of PP membranes is recommended.

Pre-Filter Cartridges

A sediment pre-filter cartridge should be utilized on all reverse osmosis units to remove large particulate substances (such as oxidized metals) from the source water before it enters the membrane housing; failing to utilize a pre-filter severely decreases the useful life of the membrane and dramatically decreases performance. An activated carbon filter is also employed in RO units, with the placement in the flow pattern determined by the material that the membrane is composed of. Activated carbon removes pesticides, dissolved organic material, and the chlorine from chlorine compounds. Note that in water containing chloramines, the molecule will be broken into chlorine and ammonia, with the chlorine becoming bound by the carbon and the ammonia passing through the membrane, as previously mentioned.

Membrane Life Span

The effective life span of a reverse osmosis membrane depends largely on the initial concentration of TDS in the source water. The higher the TDS, the faster the membrane will become impacted with material and the lower the volume of filtered water that it can produce. Hobbyists in areas of the country with exceptionally high TDS in the source water may have to replace membranes once every six months, while a hobbyist elsewhere with relatively low TDS may only have to replace the membrane once every two years, having purified the same volume of water. Back-flushing the membrane for a few minutes each week helps dislodge particles from pores and can significantly extend the life of the membrane; considering the cost of membrane replacement, this practice is strongly recommended.

The membrane should be replaced when the TDS of the permeate exceeds 5% of the source water TDS, or the rate of permeate production decreases significantly; remember, however, that the temperature of the source water will dramatically impact the permeate production rate, and that this rate is likely to decrease in the colder months of the year. Measuring the TDS of the permeate therefore becomes the primary means of determining whether or not a membrane requires replacement. Hobbyists new to reverse osmosis filtration are advised to contact the technical support personnel of the unit's manufacturer *before* buying a replacement membrane to avoid replacing it prematurely.

▲ *Is the effort to produce pure water worth it? This hammer coral under actinic lighting is a perfect answer!*

Extra Filtration

Although reverse osmosis units can remove nearly all of the contaminant substances in tap water, additional filtration through deionization resins produces some of the purest water possible. Removal rates for most substances are between 98 and 99.5%, and silica removal rates greater than 99.9% are possible with some units. In general, it may be stated that reverse osmosis units are less expensive to operate, and require less frequent maintenance, than deionization filters, a topic discussed in the following chapter.

CHAPTER 23

Deionization

Deionization involves the selective exchange of cations and anions in solution for more desirable exchangeable ions. The exchange takes place on the surface of resin beads that are made of a polymer, such as polystyrene, and subsequently activated with an agent that creates micropores on the bead surfaces. It is the size of these pores that ultimately determines the resin's capacity for ion exchange. The smaller and more numerous the pores, the greater the ion exchange capacity of the resin bead will be. Pore sizes in microporous resins are in the range of 20 to 50 Å (by contrast, macroporous resins, used to remove large molecules such as organic material from solution, feature pore sizes in the range of 200 to 500 Å). Once the pores have been created, the beads are exposed to a strong acid or base to load them with hydrogen or hydroxide ions, respectively. The result is strong acid cation and strong base anion resins.

The coating of hydrogen ions on strong acid cation resins attracts cations with a greater positive charge, such as magnesium and calcium, that pass close enough to a bead; these cations attach and knock hydrogen ions off, consequently increasing the pH of the bead. The displaced hydrogen ions enter into solution (i.e. the water). The process is essentially the same with strong base anion resins, except that anions with a greater net negative charge than the hydroxide ions coating the beads are captured, releasing the hydroxide ions into the water. In this case, the pH of the bead decreases. In the event that cation and anion exchange resins are being used to filter the same water, the hydroxide ions released into solution bond with the hydrogen ions from the cation exchange reaction and form water, as shown in Eq. 23.1.

(Eq. 23.1)

$$H^+ + OH^- \rightarrow H_2O$$

Deionization is similar in principle to water softening, however there is a difference: water softening involves the exchange of cations in solution for sodium ions. This method of ion exchange is undesirable for water purification when the express goal is to strip the water of all substances and begin with a clean slate.

Note that no waste water is produced in the deionization process. Also, the water attained from a properly maintained deionization unit can be up to 99.9% free of charged substances. Calcium, magnesium, sodium, potassium, and heavy metals account for the majority of cations that are filtered out of the source water; nitrate, bicarbonate, sulfate, chloride, and iodide are some of the more notable anions removed.

Resin Beads

Each resin bead can only capture so many ions. As the resins become exhausted, they change color as a function of pH, and this progressive color change indicates when the time has come to replace or regenerate the resins. When approximately 80 to 90% of the resin bed has changed color, the resins should be replaced or regenerated. Naturally, this is only possible if the resin cartridges are housed in transparent canisters; should opaque canisters be used, an increase in the TDS of the purified water indicates that the resins have become exhausted.

Regeneration

Cation and anion resins can be regenerated with strong acids and bases, specifically hydrochloric (muriatic) acid and caustic soda (sodium hydroxide) solution. Note

▲ *Purple sea urchin* (Arbacia punctulata) *scouring live rock for coralline algae. This species is a common hitchhiker on rock emanating from the Gulf Coast, and while interesting and beautiful, their tendency to topple corals and other sessile invertebrates, as well as their coralline algae grazing, earn them a place in a rock-filled refugium in the author's aquaria. Maintaining water chemistry parameters within a narrow range will prevent specimens such as this one from shedding their spines and eventually perishing.*

that the ion-exchange capacity of regenerated resins is lower than that of virgin resins. A qualified individual should be contracted to perform regeneration of the resins if this process is of interest to the hobbyist. Although regenerating resins is more cost effective than replacing them, it is much safer and easier to completely replace an exhausted resin canister

The diversity of marine life available to aquarists today is astounding, and with the help of modern technology, it is not a difficult task to provide them the proper environment.

with a new one. If replacing the resin, the cost of each gallon of water purified is approximately 10 cents, compared to 1 to 2 cents per gallon when regenerating the resin; in either case, purifying water via deionization is far more economical than purchasing purified water at a store.

Efficiency

The efficiency of a deionization unit is partly determined by the rate of water flow through the resin beds; if the flow is too fast, the resin won't have a long-enough contact time to properly remove undesirable ions from solution. Consequently, a flow rate of

approximately 1 gallon per minute (60 gph or 1440 gpd) or less will provide optimal filtration. The TDS of purified water should be close to 0 ppm; significantly higher TDS indicates that the water has not had sufficient contact time with the resins, therefore the hobbyist must slow the rate of water production until the TDS of the purified water becomes nearly immeasurable.

The Downside

The negative aspect of utilizing deionization resins for complete source water purification is that the volume of purified water produced by a unit varies as a function of the source water TDS—the higher the TDS, the fewer gallons of water that will be purified. Consequently, aquarists with very hard water may get only a small volume of purified water before the unit is exhausted. For this reason, the majority of hobbyists will want to utilize a combination of reverse osmosis and deionization in order to maximize the potential for water purification and longevity of the deionization resins.

Similarities to RO Membranes

Deionization resins share many points in common with reverse osmosis membranes:

- The life span of deionization resin and reverse osmosis membranes

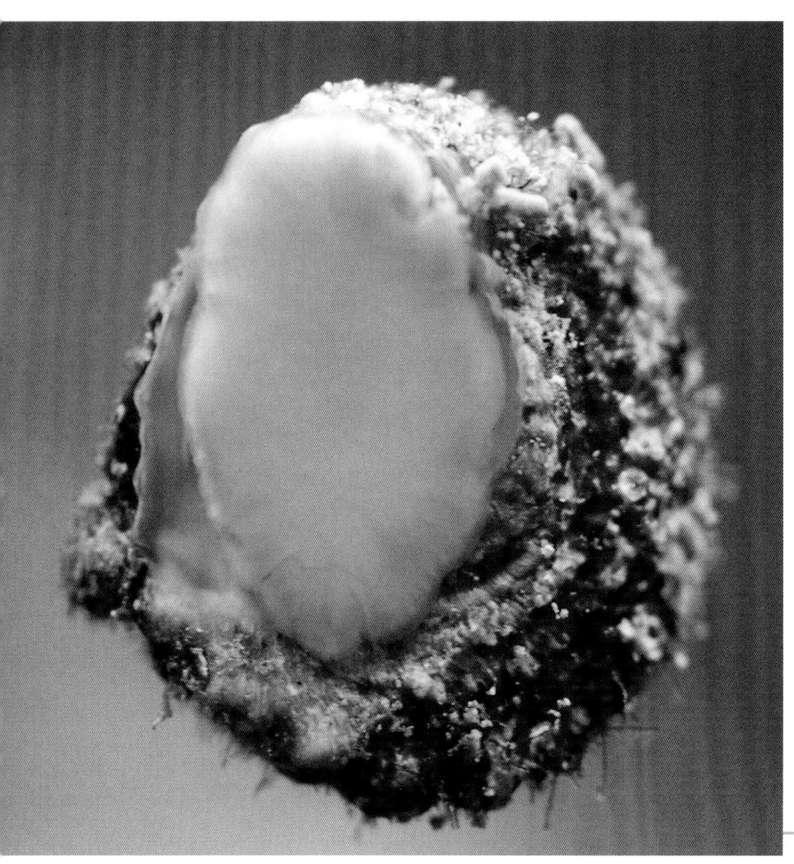

Many aquarists employ natural means to help maintain their aquaria. Snails are some of the best grazers and scavengers available to hobbyists for many reasons: they are constantly eating, they eat at the same location until all of the food is gone, they rarely squabble, and they reproduce freely in many aquaria (increasing their population and providing food for fishes). Additionally, there are a number of species available to hobbyists, many of which eat different types of algae, surface films, and detritus, and many of which exhibit different colors and shapes of their shells. Lastly, they are relatively hardy and inexpensive.

depends on the initial concentration of TDS in the tap water; the greater the TDS, the faster the resin will expire.

- A pre-filter used to remove large particulates from source water will help prolong the life of the resin.
- Hot water from the tap should never be sent through a deionization unit. Water that passes through a heating unit tends to have a higher concentration of dissolved metals (cations) relative to that of unheated water with a temperature of 70° to 77°F; passing this water through the

resin beds will cause them to expire very rapidly.

Water Quality Revisited

Parts 1 and 2 have essentially ended by returning to the beginning of the book: water quality. Typically, greater control over water quality leads to greater success as a marine aquarium hobbyist. Beginning with a clean slate upon which to build the parameters to the desired concentrations and levels creates a decided advantage, particularly in reef aquarium systems. It is for this reason that the use of reverse osmosis and/or deionization methods of water purification, regardless of whether the source water originates from a municipal treatment facility or a well, is highly recommended.

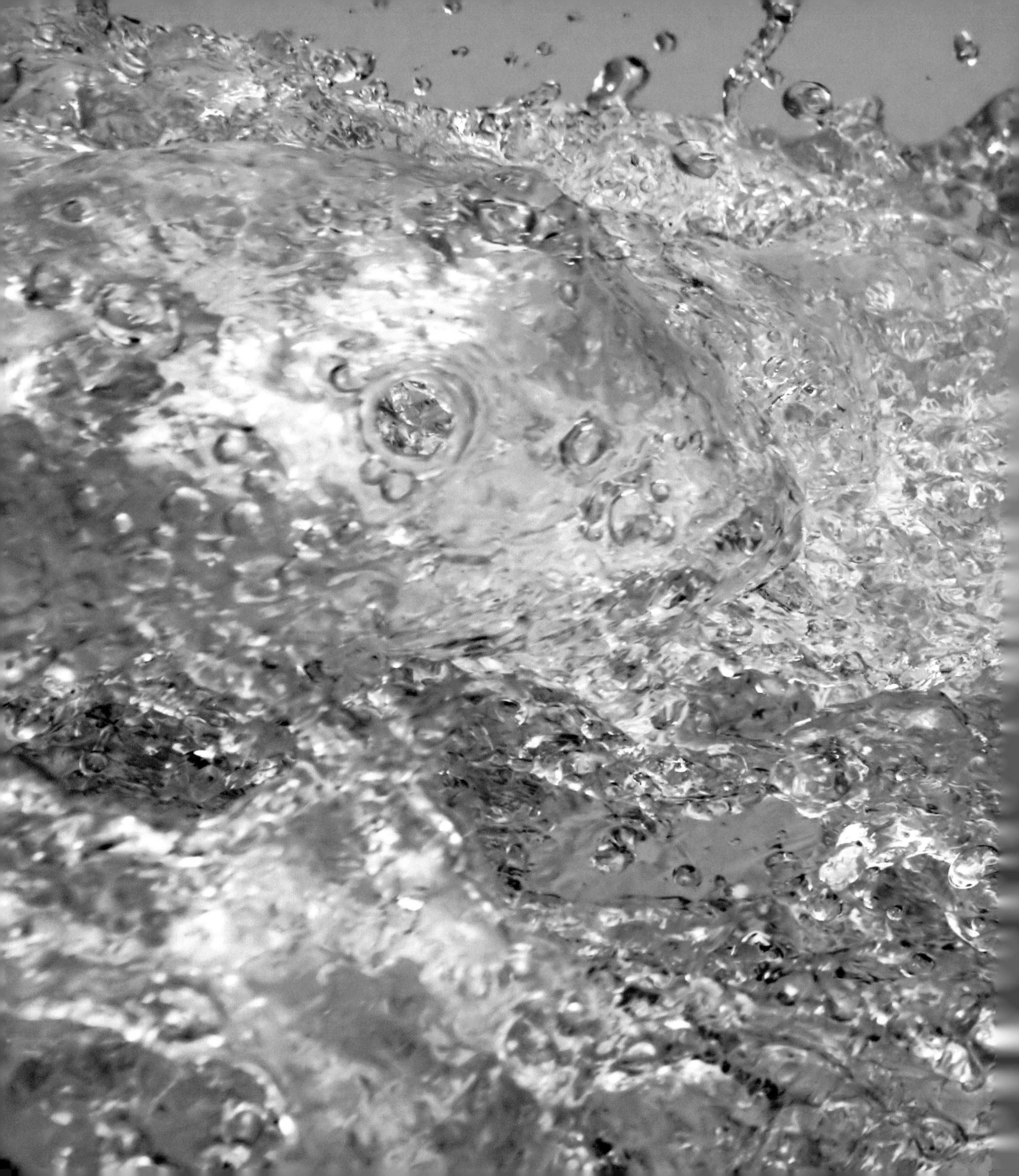

Part Three

Reference Material

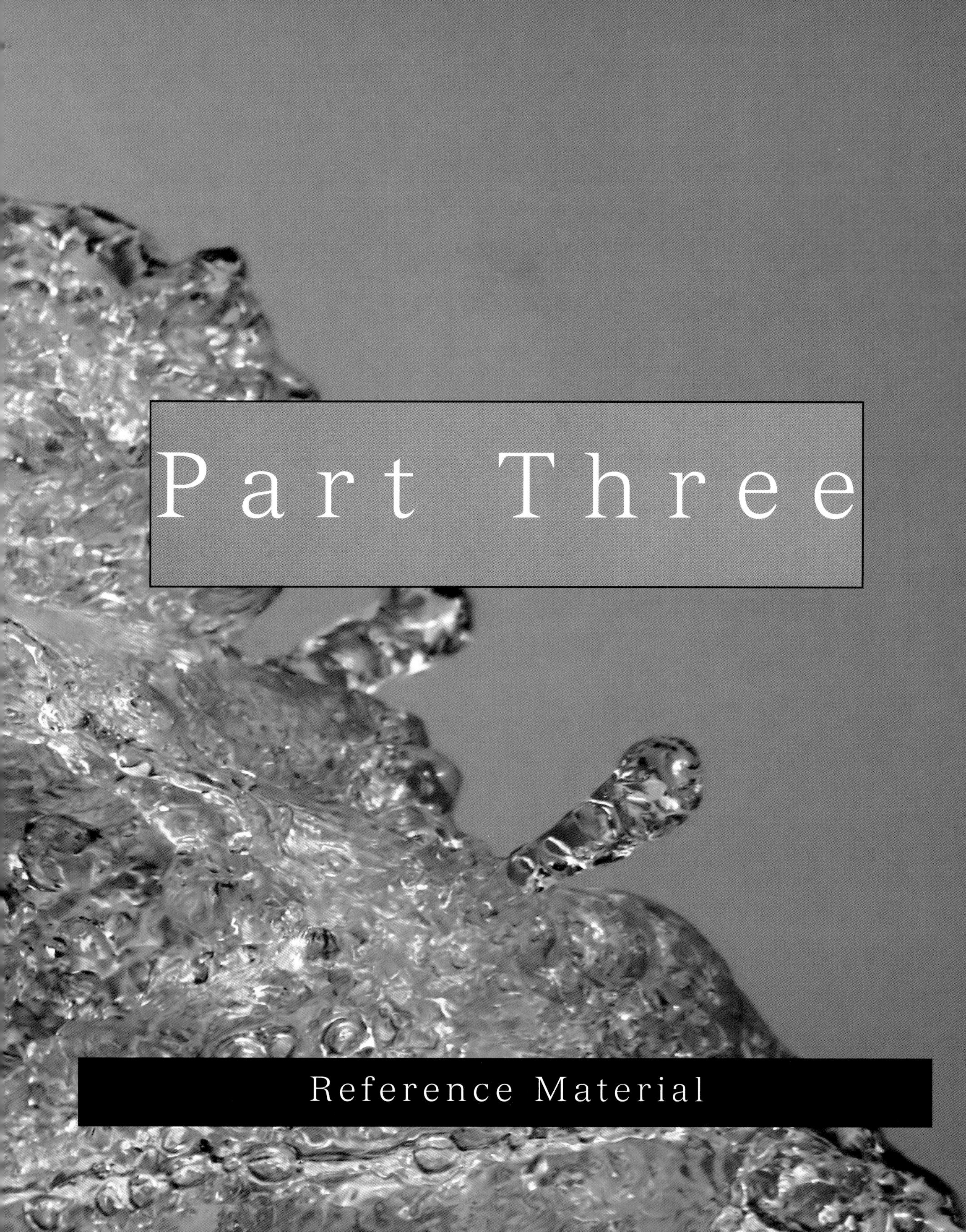

Ions and Molecules of Importance in Marine Aquaria

Conversion VII. Miscellaneous Units and Conversions

Element	Ion or Molecule	Common Name
Nitrogen	NH_3	Ammonia
	NH_4^+	Ammonium
	NO_2^-	Nitrite
	NO_3^-	Nitrate
	N_2	Nitrogen Gas
Silicon	SiO_2	Silicate, Silica
	H_4SiO_4	Silicic Acid
Sulfur	$SO4_2^-$	Sulfate
Chlorine	Cl^-	Chloride
	NaCl	Sodium Chloride
	CaCl	Calcium Chloride
	MgCl	Magnesium Chloride
	SrCl	Strontium Chloride
	KCl	Potassium Chloride
Iodine	I_2	Iodine
	I^-	Iodide

Conversion VII. Miscellaneous Units and Conversions

	IO_3^-	Iodate
Carbon	CO_2	Carbon Dioxide
	CH_4	Methane
Carbonate System	H_2CO_3	Carbonic Acid
	HCO_3^-	Bicarbonate
	CO_3^{2-}	Carbonate
	$CaCO_3$	Calcite
	$CaCO_3$	Aragonite
	$MgCO_3$	Magnesite
	$CaMg(CO_3)_2$	Dolomite
	$SrCO_3$	Strontianite
	$Cu_2CO_3(OH)_2$	Malachite
Phosphate System	PO_4^{3-}	Phosphate
	$Ca_5(PO_4)_3OH$	Hydroxylapatite
	$Mg_3(PO_4)_2 \cdot 8H_2O$	Bobierrite

Unit Conversions

Units of Volume		
1 gallon	=	3.785 L
	=	3785 cc
	=	3785 ml
1 liter	=	1000 ml
	=	1000 cc
	=	1 kg H_2O
	=	0.264172 gal.
	=	35.28 oz.
	=	33.814 fl. oz.
1 tsp	=	4.92892 ml
1 tbsp	=	14.7868 ml
1 fl. oz.	=	29.5735 ml

Units of Concentration		
1 ppT or ‰	=	ml/L
	=	3.8 ml/gal.
	=	3.8 g/gal.
	=	1 g/1000 g
	=	1 g/2.2 lbs.
1 ppm	=	1 mg/L
	=	3.8 mg/gal.
	=	1 g/m^3 H_2O
	=	1 ml/1000 ml

Units of Mass		
1 kg	=	2.20462 lbs.
1 lb.	=	0.453592 kg
1 g	=	0.035274 oz.
1 oz.	=	28.3495 g

Units of Length		
1 cm	=	0.394 in.
1 in.	=	2.54 cm

Units of Energy		
Watts	=	volts x amps
Amps	=	volts / watts
1 amp	=	120 w @ 120 V
30-amp line capacity	=	3,600 w (30 x 120)
20-amp line capacity	=	2,400 w (20 x 120)
15-amp line capacity	=	1,800 w (15 x 120)

Units of Temperature		
°C	=	(°F-32) x (5/9)
°F	=	(°C x (9/5)) +32
Kelvin	=	°C + 273.15

Miscellaneous Units and Conversions		
Alkalinity		
1 meq/L	=	50 mg/L $CaC0_3$
	=	2.8 KH
1 mg/L $CaCO_3$	=	0.02 meq/L
	=	0.056 KH
Oxygen and Carbon Dioxide		
O_2 cc/L	=	O_2 ppm x 0.7
O_2 ppm	=	O_2 cc/L x 1.429
CO_2 cc/L	=	CO_2 ppm x 0.509
CO_2 ppm	=	CO_2 cc/L x 1.964
Units of Irradiance		
lux	=	lumens/m^2 surface area
Flow Rate of a Liquid		
1 gph	=	1.05 cc/second
1 cc/second	=	0.95 gph
Weight of Water		
Freshwater (1.0 g/cm^3)		8.327 lbs./gallon
Saltwater (1.025 g/cm^3)		8.535 lbs./gallon

Periodic Table of the Elements

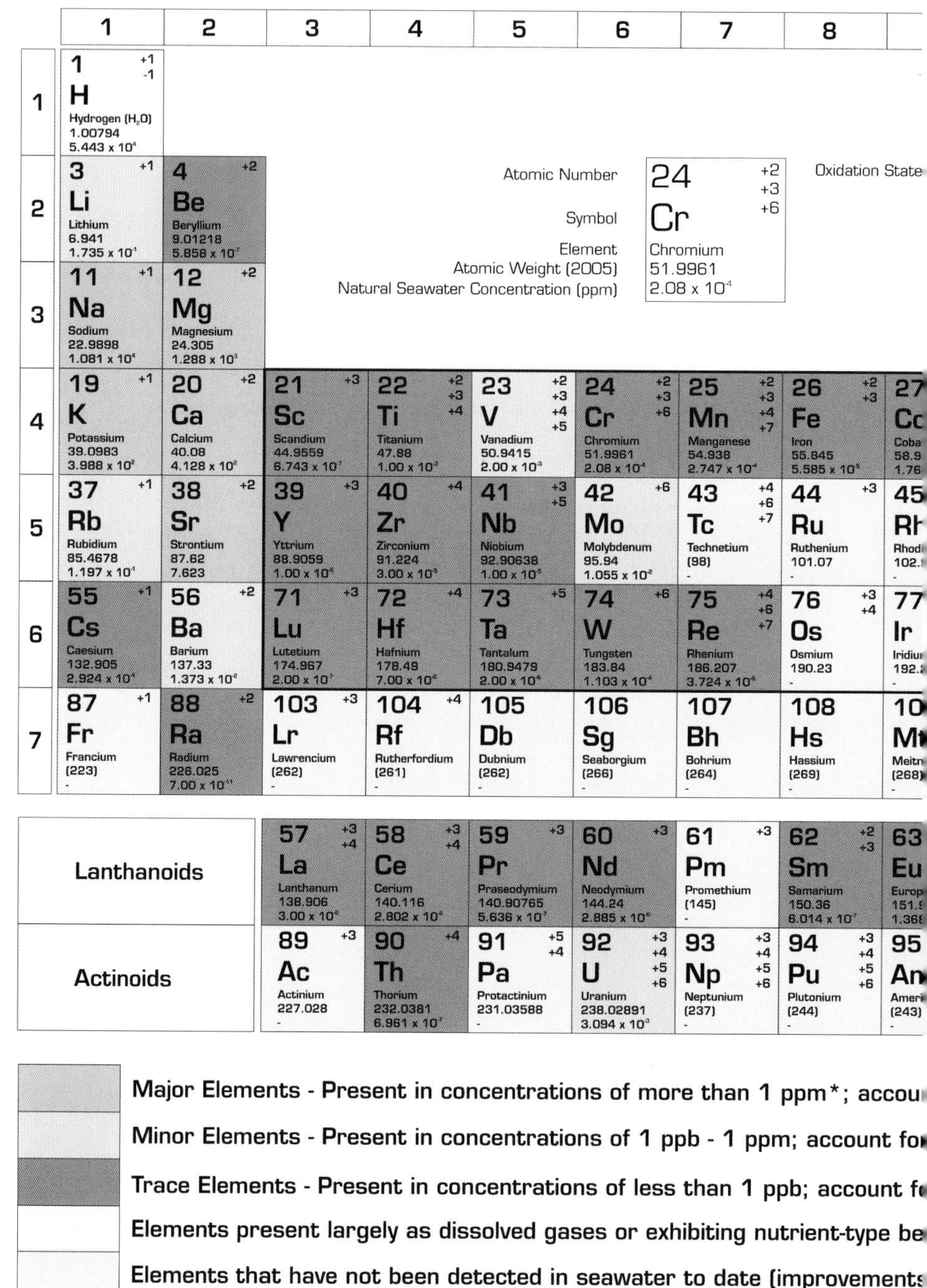

0	11	12	13	14	15	16	17	18
								2 He Helium 4.002602 7.205×10^{6}
			5 +3 B Boron 10.811 4.541	6 +2 +4 -4 C Carbon (inorg.) 12.0107 2.763×10^{1}	7 +1 - 5 -1 - 3 N Nitrogen 14.0067 11.5	8 -2 O Oxygen (diss.) 15.9994 3.520	9 -1 F Fluorine 18.9984032 1.292	10 0 Ne Neon 20.1797 1.513×10^{4}
			13 +3 Al Aluminum 26.981538 8.094×10^{4}	14 +2 +4 -4 Si Silicon 28.0855 2.809	15 +3 +6 -3 P Phosphorus 30.973761 7.124×10^{2}	16 +4 +6 -2 S Sulfur 32.065 8.978×10^{2}	17 +1 +5 +7 -1 Cl Chlorine 35.453 1.950×10^{4}	18 0 Ar Argon 39.948 5.992×10^{1}
+2 +3 0^{4}	29 +1 +2 Cu Copper 63.546 2.542×10^{4}	30 +2 Zn Zinc 65.409 3.925×10^{4}	31 +3 Ga Gallium 69.723 2.092×10^{5}	32 +2 +4 Ge Germanium 72.64 5.085×10^{6}	33 +3 +5 -3 As Arsenic 74.92160 1.723×10^{3}	34 +4 +6 -2 Se Selenium 78.96 1.342×10^{4}	35 +1 +5 -1 Br Bromine 79.904 6.712×10^{1}	36 0 Kr Krypton 83.798 2.849×10^{4}
+2 +4	47 +1 Ag Silver 107.8682 2.697×10^{6}	48 +2 Cd Cadmium 112.411 7.869×10^{5}	49 +3 In Indium 114.818 1.148×10^{7}	50 +2 +4 Sn Tin 118.71 4.748×10^{7}	51 +3 +5 -3 Sb Antimony 121.76 1.461×10^{4}	52 +4 +6 -2 Te Tellurium 127.6 -	53 +1 +5 +7 -1 I Iodine 126.90447 5.584×10^{2}	54 0 Xe Xenon 131.293 6.565×10^{5}
+2 +4	79 +1 +3 Au Gold 196.96655 4.924×10^{6}	80 +1 +2 Hg Mercury 200.59 1.003×10^{6}	81 +1 +3 Tl Thallium 204.3833 1.226×10^{5}	82 +2 +4 Pb Lead 207.2 2.072×10^{6}	83 +3 +5 Bi Bismuth 208.98038 2.090×10^{6}	84 +2 +4 Po Polonium (209) -	85 At Astatine (210) -	86 0 Rn Radon (222) -
ium	111 Rg Roentgenium (272) -	112 Uub Ununbium (285) -	113 Uut Ununtrium (284) -	114 Uuq Ununquadium (289) -	115 Uup Ununpentium (288) -	116 Uuh Ununhexium (292) -		

+3 ^{7}	65 +3 Tb Terbium 158.92534 1.430×10^{7}	66 +3 Dy Dysprosium 162.5 9.750×10^{7}	67 +3 Ho Holmium 164.93032 3.299×10^{7}	68 +3 Er Erbium 167.259 8.363×10^{7}	69 +3 Tm Thulium 168.93421 1.351×10^{7}	70 +2 +3 Yb Ytterbium 173.04 8.652×10^{7}
+3	97 +3 +4 Bk Berkelium (247) -	98 +3 Cf Californium (251) -	99 +3 Es Einsteinium (252) -	100 +3 Fm Fermium (257) -	101 +2 +3 Md Mendelevium (258) -	102 +2 +3 No Nobelium (259) -

9.9% of total dissolved substances in seawater.

f total dissolved substances in seawater.

6 of total dissolved substances in seawater.

ng them to be excluded from the list of Major Elements by many authors.

methods may eventually change this);

APPENDIX
Calculations

Carrying out Important Chemical Calculations

Calculating the Amount of a Supplement Required to Obtain a Specific Ionic Concentration

Hobbyists often want to know how much of a certain product is required to increase the concentration of some ion in their aquarium to obtain a target value. Although it seems like a complex task, making the required calculations generally takes no more than a few minutes and will enable hobbyists to exercise greater control over the chemical parameters of their systems than when simply following a manufacturer's directions. While performing these calculations might not necessarily increase a hobbyist's success rate or greatly improve the appearance of the aquarium, it's reasonable to assert that the more informed a hobbyist becomes, the better the decisions they will make in terms of quality products such as additives and salt mixes. For those hobbyists interested in controlling such parameters as calcium, magnesium, strontium, iodide, and carbonate hardness to the greatest possible extent, being able to perform the following calculations is not an option—it's the only way to obtain accurate initial concentrations.

Regular water testing with accurate kits over a prolonged period of time enables the hobbyist to chart the rates of uptake of the target ion species, and therefore dictates the frequency with which a substance of a given strength or concentration must be added to the system in order to maintain a concentration within the desired range. For example, maintaining the calcium concentration in an aquarium by solely relying upon the directions on a calcium supplement's label often leads to a see-saw effect in which significant time is spent trying to attain a stable reading, but which often leads to frustration. By knowing how much of the supplement to add on a daily basis, a stock solution can be created that is simple to administer and will faithfully maintain the concentration during periods of general chemical stability. In fact, if the entirety of the water in the aquarium is considered to constitute the solution and the hobbyist knows what the concentration of some substance needs to be (i.e. the calcium concentration should be approximately 412 mg/L, or 0.412%) and also knows the rate of consumption, it's a simple task to determine the rate of supplement addition required to attain and maintain this concentration.

Because maintaining the calcium concentration in reef aquaria is one of the main areas of focus, this scenario makes a constructive example with which to illustrate the process of calculation. To determine the amount of a supplement required to obtain a desired concentration in the aquarium water, the initial concentration of the substance in the raw ingredient must be known. This in turn depends on whether the raw ingredient is in the form of a solid or is already in solution (aqueous). We'll look at both cases. In the first, calcium chloride in the solid form will be used as the calcium source, and in the second, a calcium chloride solution with a concentration of 100,000 mg/L is used. (The concentration of the solution should be stated somewhere on the product's label).

Step 1

The first step is to determine the concentration of calcium in the aquarium system by testing it. For this example, assume that the aquarium system contains 100 gallons of water (taking into account the volume of the aquarium and sump, as well as water displacement from live rock and aragonite sand) and currently has a residual calcium concentration of 300 mg/L, and that the intention is to gradually increase it to the natural seawater concentration of 412 mg/L.

Since $[Ion_{Desired}] - [Ion_{Actual}] = [Ion_{Required}]$ this means that an additional 112 mg/L of ionic calcium is required to obtain the desired concentration:
$412mg\ Ca^{2+} \cdot L^{-1} - 300mg\ Ca^{2+} \cdot L^{-1} = 112mg\ Ca^{2+} \cdot L^{-1}$

Step 2
Convert the actual volume of water in the aquarium from gallons into liters.
(1 US gallon = 3.785 L)

Since Gallons in Entire Aquarium System x 3.785 L·gal-1 = Liters in Entire Aquarium System, we have 100 gallons x 3.785 L·gal-1 = 3,785 Liters

Step 3
To determine the overall mass of calcium needed to increase the concentration by 112 mg/L (in this example), multiply that value by the volume of water in the system in liters.

Since $[Ion_{Req'd}]$ x Liters in Entire Aquarium System = mg Ions Req'd, we need
$112mg\ Ca^{2+} \cdot L^{-1} \times 3785\ L = 423{,}920mg\ Ca^{2+}$

Step 4
The required amount of calcium may seem excessive until you remember that the unit of measurement, mg, is quite small. Convert this unit to grams by dividing it by 1,000 (1 gram consists of 1,000 mg).
Milligrams Ions Req'd ÷ 1000 = Grams Ions Req'd, or $423{,}920mg\ Ca^{2+} \div 1000 = 423.920g\ Ca^{2+}$

In this example, 423.92 grams (just shy of 1 pound) of *actual calcium* is required to make the desired change. This is not to say that all the calcium should be added at once, nor that 424 grams of some calcium supplement will accomplish the goal (remember that only a percentage of any supplement is actually made up of the target ion species). Chapter 8 illustrated that calcium chloride, for example, is approximately 35% calcium. This percentage is determined by using the atomic weight of the ions in the molecule, which can be found on the periodic table of the elements in Appendix I. To determine the amount of a substance present in a molecule, take the sum of atoms of each substance in the molecule and multiply them by the atomic weight of that element; then add these products to get the overall weight of the molecule. Each molecule of calcium chloride ($CaCl_2$) is composed of one calcium ion and a pair of chloride ions.

Steps 5 through 7 need only be followed if the percentage of the active ingredient (in this case, calcium) is either unknown or not listed on the label; otherwise, skip to Step 8.

Step 5

Sum (Number of Atoms in Molecule x Atomic Weight of that Element) = Molecular $\text{Weight}_{\text{Total}}$

Molecular $\text{Weight}_{\text{Total}}$			
Molecule	$CaCl_2$		
Element	# Atoms	Atomic Weight	Total Mass in Molecule
Ca	1	40.078	40.078
Cl	2	35.453	70.906
			110.984

Step 6

Divide the total mass of the target element (calcium in our example) by the total molecular weight to get the percentage of mass that the element comprises in that molecule.

Target $\text{Element}_{\text{Atomic Weight Total}}$ ÷ Molecular $\text{Weight}_{\text{Total}}$ = Target $\text{Element}_{\text{Percentage by Weight}}$

40.078 ÷ 110.984 = 0.361

In this case, roughly 36.1% of calcium chloride is composed of calcium.

Step 7

Very few chemicals are completely pure; impurities and contaminants such as water, silicate, or trace metals are often present in a chemical and account for a percentage of the mass.

The highest grades of calcium chloride are typically 98% pure, meaning that 2% or so of the chemical is composed of other substances. Factor this percentage of purity into the equation by multiplying it by the percentage of the target element.

Again, to find out the purity of the product, contact the manufacturer. They may not be willing to share this information, though, as it may be considered proprietary. If this is the case, the hobbyist may do some Internet research into the likely purity of the product, or he may simply choose the product of a manufacturer willing to disclose the information.

% of Element in Molecule x % of Chemical Purity = % of Active Element in Supplement
0.361 x 0.98 = 0.354 or 35.4% Ca^{2+}

The calculation illustrates that approximately 35%, as opposed to 36%, of the total mass of the chemical is actually composed of calcium. The 1% discrepancy difference might not seem like much, but when large amounts of a chemical need to be added to the aquarium to make up for a deficiency, the magnitude of the difference becomes more evident. The reason for this is quite simple: unless the percentage of impurity is factored in, the amount of chemical needed will be lower than is actually required, which means that a greater amount of the chemical would be required to increase the concentration to the desired level than was initially calculated.

Step 8

Next, use the percentage of active ingredient to calculate the actual mass of the chemical required to obtain the desired increase in concentration. To do this, divide the total mass of the target element needed (calculated in Step 4) by the percentage calculated in Step 7 or taken from the label.

Grams of Ions Req'd ÷ Overall % of Target Element in Supplement = Total Mass of Supplement Req'd

423.920g Ca^{2+} ÷ 0.354g Ca^{2+} [in 1g $CaCl_2$] = 1197.514g of Calcium Chloride

Now that the calculations have indicated the amount of calcium chloride required to increase the calcium concentration by 112 mg/L, the decision over which form of the chemical is the most sensible to use (solid or aqueous) can be made.

Step 8a—Using Solid $CaCl_2$

Using solid $CaCl_2$ requires the amount calculated in Step 8. Since approximately 1,198 grams (about 2.6 pounds) of calcium chloride is required, it certainly makes sense from an economical standpoint to buy it as a solid (powder or pellets, depending on the manufacturer) and mix it with purified water to form a stock solution that can be added daily. Note that adding a chemical to an aquarium too rapidly can cause unwanted precipitation reactions with other ions in the aquarium (notably carbonates, in this case), which can cause a dip in alkalinity and fluctuations in pH.

Step 8b—Using a $CaCl_2$ Solution

Suppose, however, that a powdered calcium chloride supplement is unavailable at the local aquarium shop, and all they carry is calcium chloride in solution. Hopefully, the label lists the calcium concentration of the product, either by percentage or mg/L. That information can be used to determine the volume of the product required to reach the target calcium concentration. In this example, a product with a calcium concentration of 10%, or 100,000 mg/L, will be used, so each liter of solution contains 100,000 mg of calcium. The total mass of calcium required is 423,920 mg. Therefore, to determine the total volume of solution needed to provide this mass, divide the value by the strength of the calcium solution.

Total Mass of Target Element Req'd ÷ Strength of Sol'n = Volume of Sol'n Req'd

423,920mg Ca^{2+} ÷ 100,000mg $Ca^{2+} \cdot L^{-1}$ = 4.2392 L of calcium chloride solution

So 4.2392 L (1.1198 gallons) of the calcium supplement must be added to increase the concentration in the system to the desired level.

Powdered supplements are always considerably less expensive than liquid products because they contain no water, making them less expensive to ship from the manufacturer to the distributor and dealer. Also, they treat a greater volume of aquarium water by weight than liquid solutions. If a 200-g jar of calcium chloride contains roughly 71 g of calcium and a 250-ml bottle of calcium solution with a concentration of 100,000 mg/L contains 25 g of calcium, and the products retail for $7 and $5 respectively, the hobbyist is paying 10 cents per gram of calcium in the powder and 20 cents per gram of calcium in the solution. In this example, it's clear to see that the powdered product is far more economical than the solution.

As previously stated, increasing the calcium concentration on this level of magnitude must be done gradually.

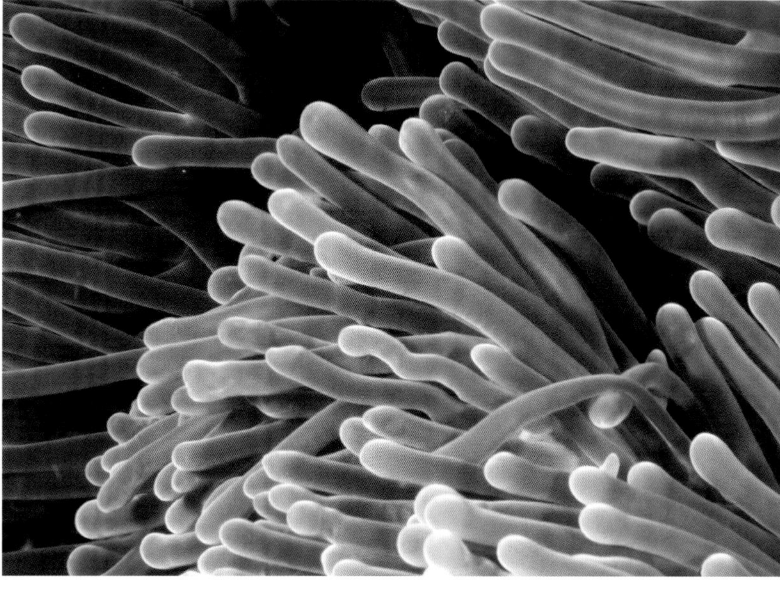

Do not dump 3 pounds of calcium chloride into the aquarium and walk away. Rather, the process will take several weeks. During this time, corals and other reef-building organisms will be extracting calcium from the water. That being the case, it will take more calcium to reach the target value than has been calculated. If the aquarium has been tested on a daily basis and the average rate of calcium consumption in the system has been determined, the amount of extra calcium additive required to reach the target concentration in the same span of time can be calculated.

Step 9

Once the desired concentration has been reached, the hobbyist may then use the observed daily rate of consumption to calculate the amount of the supplement required on a daily basis to maintain this concentration to within a small margin of error. In keeping with the example, assume that the daily rate of calcium consumption is 2 mg/L. The total amount of calcium consumed on a daily basis in this aquarium is calculated as follows.

Liters in Entire Aquarium System x Daily Decrease in Concentration = mg Target Ion Req'd·Day^{-1}

3785 Liters x 2mg Ca^{2+}·L^{-1}·Day^{-1} = 7570mg Ca^{2+}·Day^{-1} = 7.570g Ca^{2+}·Day^{-1}

Using this calculation, the amount of daily calcium supplementation required can now be determined by knowing the active strength of the supplement being used. Again, calcium chloride will be used as the supplement, since the necessary calculations have been performed.

Step 9a—Using Solid $CaCl_2$

Recall that the active strength of a powdered calcium chloride supplement, taking impurities into account, is 35.4%. The total mass of the powdered supplement required per day can be calculated as follows.

Grams of Target Ion Req'd·Day^{-1} ÷ % of Active Element in Supplement = Grams of Supplement Req'd·Day^{-1}

7.570g Ca^{2+}·Day^{-1} ÷ 35.4% = 21.384g Calcium-Chloride·Day^{-1}

Step 9b—Using $CaCl_2$ Solution

The result of the previous calculations shows that a total of 21.384 g of calcium chloride must be added on a daily basis to make up for calcium depletion; however, with a solution the active strength of the supplement must be known in order to calculate the daily dosing requirement.

Milligrams of Target Ion Req'd·Day^{-1} x Strength of Sol'n = Volume of Sol'n Req'd

7,570mg Ca^{2+}·Day^{-1} ÷ 100,000mg Ca^{2+}·L^{-1} = 0.0757 L of Calcium Chloride Solution·Day^{-1}

The total daily volume of the solution required to maintain the calcium concentration is 0.0757 L, or 75.7 ml. At this rate, a hobbyist would be using an 8-oz. bottle of the solution every three days or so, which forces him to take one of the following courses of action:

- Begin buying the solution in bulk sizes
- Switch from current product to a stronger solution
- Switch from the solution to a powdered supplement

Understanding and knowing how to perform the calculations presented in this section will take a great deal of the guesswork out of supplementation. Putting this knowledge to proper use relies on the attention paid to making precise measurements and having accurate test kits on hand. As noted in Chapter 19, test kit reliability and accuracy are of paramount importance; purchasing inaccurate test kits is a waste of money. One cannot intelligently maintain water parameters without knowing what the parameters are!

APPENDIX
Chemical Reactions

Chemical Reactions Referenced Throughout the Text

7.1: Ammonia/Ammonium Equilibrium*
$H_2O_{(l)} + NH_{3(aq)} \leftrightarrow NH_4^+{}_{(aq)} + OH^-{}_{(aq)}$

7.2: Denitrification
$(CH_2O)_{106}(NH_3)_{16}H_3O_4 + 84.8\ HNO_3 \leftrightarrow 148.8\ H_2O + 106\ CO_2 + 42.4\ N_2 + 16\ NH_3 + H_3PO_4$

7.3: Sulfate Reduction
$(CH_2O)_{106}(NH_3)_{16}H_3PO_4 + 53\ SO_4^{2-} \rightarrow 106\ CO_2 + 106\ H_2O + 16\ NH_3 + 53\ S^{2-} + H_3PO_4$

8.1: Calcium Carbonate Equilibrium**
$CaCO_{3(s)} \leftrightarrow Ca^{2+}{}_{(aq)} + CO_3^{2-}{}_{(aq)}$

8.2: Carbonate/Bicarbonate Equilibrium*
$H^+{}_{(aq)} + CO_3^{2-}{}_{(aq)} \leftrightarrow HCO_3^-{}_{(aq)}$

8.3: Bicarbonate/Carbonic Acid Equilibrium*
$HCO_3^-{}_{(aq)} + H^+{}_{(aq)} \leftrightarrow H_2CO_{3(aq)}$

8.4: Carbonic Acid Equilibrium
$CO_{2(g)} + H_2O_{(l)} \leftrightarrow H_2CO_{3(aq)}$

8.5: Formation of Apatite (Bonding of Aqueous Calcium with Phosphate)
$3\ Ca^{2+} + 2\ PO_4^{3-} \leftrightarrow Ca_3(PO_4)_2$

8.6: Calcium Chloride Equilibrium**
$CaCl_{2(aq)} \leftrightarrow Ca^{2+}{}_{(aq)} + 2Cl^-{}_{(aq)}$

8.7: Formation of Calcium Carbonate**
$Ca^{2+}{}_{(aq)} + CO_3^{2-}{}_{(aq)} \leftrightarrow CaCO_{3(s)}$

9.1: Strontium Chloride Equilibrium**
$SrCl_{2(aq)} \leftrightarrow Sr^{2+}{}_{(aq)} + 2Cl^-{}_{(aq)}$

9.2: Strontium Carbonate Equilibrium**

$Sr^{2+}_{(aq)} + CO_3^{2-}_{(aq)} \leftrightarrow SrCO_{3(s)}$

10.1: Magnesium Carbonate Equilibrium**

$Mg^{2+}_{(aq)} + CO_3^{2-}_{(aq)} \leftrightarrow MgCO_{3(s)}$

11.1: Photosynthesis, Simplified

$6\ CO_2 + 6\ H_2O \xrightarrow[\text{light energy}]{} C_6H_{12}O_6 + 6\ O_2$

11.2: Formation of Iodate†

$3\ O_2 + 2\ I^- \rightarrow 2\ IO_3^-$

13.1: Formation of Organic Material via Photosynthesis

$106\ CO_2 + 122\ H_2O + 16\ HNO_3 + \underbrace{H_3PO_4}_{\text{phosphate utilized}} \leftrightarrow$

$\underbrace{(CH_2O)_{106}(NH_3)_{16}H_3PO_4}_{\text{organic matter produced}} + 138\ O_2$

13.2: Aerobic Decomposition of Organic Material††

$(CH_2O)_{106}(NH_3)_{16}H_3PO_4 + 138\ O_2 \leftrightarrow$
organic matter utilized
$106\ CO_2 + 122\ H_2O + 16\ HNO_3 + H_3PO_4$
phosphate produced

15.1: Formation of Ozone

$O_2 + O \rightarrow O_3$

23.1: Formation of Water from Residual Hydrogen and Hydroxide Ions During Deionization

$H^+ + OH^- \leftrightarrow H_2O$

Other Chemical Reactions of Importance in Marine Aquaria

Carbonic Acid Formation in Systems with Poor Degassing Capabilities

$CO_{2(g)} + H_2O_{(l)} \rightarrow H_2CO_{3(aq)}$

Dissociation of Carbonic Acid, Resulting in the Liberation of Free Hydrogen Ions

$H_2CO_{3(aq)} \rightarrow HCO_3^-{}_{(aq)} + H^+{}_{(aq)}$

Dissociation of Bicarbonate, Resulting in the Liberation of Free Hydrogen Ions

$HCO_3^-{}_{(aq)} \rightarrow H^+{}_{(aq)} + CO_3^{2-}{}_{(aq)}$

Formation of Calcium Carbonate in Systems with Abundant Free Carbonate Ions

$Ca^{2+}{}_{(aq)} + CO_3^{2-}{}_{(aq)} \rightarrow CaCO_{3(s)}$

Calcium Hydroxide Equilibrium

$Ca(OH)_{2(s)} \leftrightarrow Ca^{2+}{}_{(aq)} + 2\ OH^-{}_{(aq)}$

pH-neutralizing Effect of Free Hydroxide Ions

$H^+{}_{(aq)} + OH^-{}_{(aq)} \rightarrow H_2O_{(l)}$

*Reactions so denoted are directly driven by pH.

**Some reactions are driven by such variables as temperature, pressure, and the percent saturation of the solution, and while pH of the solution may play a role in the rate of the reaction, it is a smaller influence than these variables. A reaction is said to be in equilibrium when the rates of dissolution and precipitation are equal (denoted by the "↔" between the two halves of the reaction).

For those not familiar with the chemical notation following the ions and molecules, "(aq)" indicates that the substance is in the "aqueous" form, meaning that it's dissolved in water (i.e., $Ca^{2+}{}_{(aq)}$ denotes a calcium ion dissolved in water); "(s)" indicates that the substance is in the form of a solid; and "(l)" indicates that the substance is in liquid form.

†Molecules containing multiple oxygen atoms, such as iodate, sulfate, and nitrate, are naturally reduced by bacteria in low-oxygen environments. The formation of these molecules may be attributed to natural oxidation (in the case of iodate) or to formation as a product of some other reaction (in the case of nitrate).

††Decomposition reactions take place as the organic molecules are consumed by heterotrophic organisms such as fungi, bacteria, and protozoans.

Afterword

There may be no hobby so relaxing, and possibly frustrating, as the care of an aquarium, be it freshwater, brackish, or marine in nature. This is a challenging hobby, not a routine or task, which requires a desire to learn about chemistry, biology, physics, and animal behavior in order to achieve success. A positive aspect of aquarium husbandry is that the overall health of the inhabitants and appearance of aquarium are largely visual affirmations of a hobbyist's knowledge and dedication; the rewards justify the means.

The topic of conservation in the marine environment, particularly with respect to tropical reefs, has been quite a hotbed in the past two decades, and it will undoubtedly continue to be so with the passage of time. Many environmental activists and lobbyists are opposed to people keeping domestic dogs and cats in their homes, so one can imagine how some environmentalists feel about aquaria stocked with wild-caught fish, invertebrates, and live rock. It is prudent to mention that most reef-destructive activities are the result of dragging nets meant to capture food fish along the reef face. At the time of this writing, several facilities around the world are dedicated to developing and facilitating the captive breeding and propagation of ornamental marine fishes and invertebrates, and a great many of them also farm their own live rock by seeding reef areas with rock from other locales and then harvesting them after a period of months for sale in the hobby. Although it may be some time before such facilities are able to supply the entire demand of the marine aquarium hobby, they are doing more and more with each passing day to lighten the burden that livestock collection places on reefs. The day may come when marine aquarium hobbyists are called upon to restock the reefs with life that they have helped remove from them. Even after that day arrives, it will always be up to each hobbyist to responsibly care for the animals they place in their systems, thereby exerting as little influence as possible on the sometimes delicate balance that exists on a reef. A hobbyist who continues to learn about marine life and its care will always be improving upon his or her understanding of the big picture.

It is my express wish that this book has addressed many issues of interest to hobbyists pertaining to relevant aspects of marine water chemistry, and above all, that the information has been presented in a clear manner. I have enjoyed writing extensively on this subject and hope that the contribution made to aquarium literature continues to be useful for many years to come. Enjoy your marine aquarium!

Kindest regards to all,
Chris Brightwell, 2006

Glossary

Abiogenic: Reference to a substance which is not produced by living organisms.

Activated Carbon: Particulate carbon material which has been made porous via chemical- or heat-induced means in order to create sites for the binding of dissolved substances in solution.

Aerobic: Indicating a biological reaction that takes place in the presence of oxygen.

Alkalinity: In general terms, the sum of the concentrations of substances in solution that offset changes in pH via neutralization of acid bearing substances; carbonate and bicarbonate ions are principally responsible for this acid neutralization. In the context of aquarium husbandry, alkalinity equates to the relative stability of the pH. More formally, alkalinity is the molar concentration of the net negative charge of carbonate and bicarbonate ions in solution, expressed as milliequivalents per liter (meq/L).

Ammonia: A molecule composed of one nitrogen atom and three hydrogen atoms, with the empirical formula NH_3. In aquatic environments, ammonia is produced by the degradation of dissolved organic nitrogen by heterotrophic bacteria.

Ammonification: The reaction in which ammonia bonds with hydrogen ions (H^+) or water molecules (H_2O) to form ammonium (NH_4^+).

Ammonium: A molecule composed of one nitrogen atom and four hydrogen atoms, the fourth proton giving the molecule an overall charge of +1, with the empirical formula NH_4^+. In aquatic environments, ammonium is produced by the process of ammonification.

Anaerobic: Indicating a biological reaction that takes place in the absence of oxygen.

Aragonite: A mineral composed primarily of calcium and carbonate, with impurities including magnesium, strontium, potassium, and numerous trace elements. Aragonite is a form of the mineral calcite that is less stable at standard temperature and pressure, and therefore is more soluble (and less abundant) than calcite. Aragonite forms both biogenically and abiogenically.

Autotrophic: A method of metabolism in which energy is obtained from the oxidation of inorganic nutrient sources.

Bioaccumulation: The gradual buildup of a substance in the tissues or skeletal components of living organisms with time caused by inability to excrete or rid the body of the substance.

Biocide: A substance that is toxic to living organisms. Chlorine and chloramines are biocides commonly encountered by aquarium hobbyists.

Biofilm: A layer of microorganisms that have colonized some surface; the layer typically displays variations in structure and is composed of genetically-diverse organisms, which creates the potential for numerous types of reactions and community interactions to take place.

Biogenic: Reference to a substance which is produced by living organisms.

Biointermediate Element: An element that is utilized in biological reactions but whose concentration does not vary as a result of the abundance of the element in the system.

Biolimiting: A substance that must be present in some concentration or abundance in order for biological processes to proceed. The concentration of biolimiting substances may be affected by biological, chemical, and/or geological processes.

Biomagnification: The process in which the concentration of a substance gradually increases in the tissues of progressively higher trophic level consumers. Organisms at the highest trophic level have the greatest concentration of toxins as a result of this process.

Biouptake: The passive or active uptake of substances by living organisms.

Calcite: A mineral composed primarily of calcium and carbonate, with impurities including magnesium, strontium, potassium, and numerous trace elements. Calcite is more thermodynamically stable, therefore is less soluble, than aragonite (a different crystalline structure of the same mineral). Calcite forms both biogenically and abiogenically.

Calcium Carbonate: $CaCO_3$. A molecule composed of one calcium ion and one carbonate ion; pure calcium carbonate is approximately 39% calcium by dry weight. It is also largely insoluble in water under conditions normally found within marine aquaria, limiting its usefulness as a calcium supplement without altering the chemical environment (specifically, the pH) within a reaction chamber.

Calcium Chloride: $CaCl_2$. A molecule composed of one calcium ion and a pair of chloride ions; pure calcium chloride is approximately 36% calcium by dry weight (it is more likely to be 35% of lower as a result of common chemical impurities). It is largely soluble in water and is a commonly-used source of calcium in reef aquaria.

Calcium EDTA: $C_{10}H_{12}CaN_2Na_2O_8$. A molecule composed of one calcium ion and one EDTA molecule (ethylenediaminetetraacetic acid); calcium EDTA is approximately 11% calcium by dry weight, with the remaining 89% of the molecule attributable to the organic component. This aspect of calcium EDTA makes it a poor choice as a calcium source in marine aquaria.

Calcium Gluconate: $(CH_2OH(CHOH)_4COO)_2Ca$. A molecule composed of one calcium ion and two gluconate molecules; calcium gluconate is approximately 9% calcium by dry weight, the remainder being attributable to the organic component. The combination of low solubility and high organic content make calcium gluconate a particularly poor choice for use as a calcium source in marine aquaria.

Calcium Hydroxide: $Ca(OH)_2$. A molecule composed of one calcium ion and a pair of hydroxide ions; calcium hydroxide is approximately 51% calcium by dry weight, and is known in marine aquarium circles by its

German name, Kalkwasser. Low solubility of calcium hydroxide and its tendency to rapidly increase the pH of a solution often limit its use as a calcium source in marine aquaria.

Calcium Reactor: A vessel in which calcareous media is dissolved in a controlled fashion by lowering the pH and adjusting the rate of water flow through the vessel. pH within the vessel is usually lowered via the controlled injection of carbon dioxide, however it may also be accomplished with sulfate injection. The resulting effluent is rich in calcium, carbonate, and the other constituents of the media, and is utilized to dose these elements to the aquarium.

Carbonate Hardness: See Alkalinity.

Cellulose Acetate (CA): A material used to form reverse osmosis membranes. Susceptible to biofouling by microbes present in water, therefore requires that the incoming water be treated by some means (such as chlorination and/or chloramination) to prohibit the colonization of these organisms in the membrane itself.

Cellulose Triacetate (CTA): A type of CA membrane material.

Chelate: The process of binding a substance, most often a cation, with a molecule (which may or may not be organic in nature) in order to create a stable complex. In seawater, chelation of a cation with a molecule such as EDTA prevents the precipitation of the cation with anions in solution; this is of particular importance for trace and minor elements, many of which have a tendency to oxidize in solution to form highly-insoluble metal-oxide compounds.

Chloramine: A molecule created by combining chlorine gas and liquefied ammonia in water; the resultant compound is utilized as a biocide to treat drinking water.

Chlorine: In aquarium context, a diatomic gas composed of pairs of chlorine atoms joined with covalent bonds, administered to drinking water supplies as a biocide.

Colloidal Silica: Colloidal silica is that which has become bound with multiple additional silica molecules, organic material, or complex inorganic molecules (typically featuring calcium). In this form, it remains suspended in solution and is not reactive.

Colorimetric: Chemical analysis that relies on the color of a sample changing in order to express the value of the target substance.

Concentrate: In the context of reverse osmosis water purification, the water that contains the substances rejected by the reverse osmosis membrane.

Conservative Behavior: Indicates that the concentration of the element in question is not impacted by biological processes but rather is controlled by physical processes. All major elements are considered conservative.

Covalent Bond: A bond between two or more ions in which electrons are shared.

Crossflow: Referring to the parallel path that the concentrate follows with respect to the membrane material in reverse osmosis water purification.

Cyanobacteria: A phylum of bacteria that obtain energy via photosynthesis; commonly referred to as "slime algae" or "blue-green algae" in aquarium context, although they are not algae at all. One of the oldest and most important groups of organisms on Earth in terms of their ability to reduce atmospheric concentrations of carbon dioxide and liberate free oxygen.

Deionization: Also known as ion exchange, the process of selectively replacing undesirable cations and anions in solution with hydrogen and hydroxide ions, respectively.

Denitrification: The biological process whereby nitrate is reduced to nitrogen gas; carried out by heteretrophic bacteria in low-oxygen environments.

Denitrifier: Reference to the microbes responsible for the process of denitrification.

Detrivore: An organism that obtains food from the consumption of decaying particulate organic material (detritus).

Diatoms: A group of phytoplankton whose shells are composed of silica. In the open ocean, diatoms take in nutrients more rapidly than any other group of phytoplankton. The concentration of dissolved silica in seawater limits their productivity (hence their rates of growth and reproduction), and therefore it is directly linked to overall marine productivity.

Dichloramine: One of the three inorganic forms that chloramines take; each dichloramine molecule possesses two chloride ions.

Dissolved Organic Matter (DOM): The organic matter in seawater that is present in a dissolved form as opposed to being particulate; the criteria that define material as being dissolved is that it must be able to pass through a sieve possessing 0.4μm pores.

Distillation: A process of water purification in which the water is heated until it becomes steam, and is then allowed to collect on a surface or within a container. Because most contaminants (organic or inorganic) in the water will not vaporize, they are left in the heating vessel. Distillation is considered to be a very effective means of water purification.

EPA: Environmental Protection Agency.

Feed Channel Spacer: In reverse osmosis membranes, the layer of material between adjoining membrane layers that allows the passage of the concentrate out of the membrane housing.

Filtrate: See Permeate.

General Hardness: A misrepresentation of the abbreviation GH, from Gesamthaerte, translated from German to mean "total hardness;" the sum of the divalent cations (but primarily calcium and magnesium) in solution. Applicable to freshwater aquaria, but of no relevance to marine aquaria.

Heavy Metal: Those trace elements with an atomic weight greater than 20 atomic mass units (amu).

Heterotrophic: A method of metabolism in which energy is obtained from the consumption of organic nutrient sources.

Hydrated: In the context of this text, the binding of water molecules to ions or molecules as a result of ionic interactions.

Hydrated Silica (Biogenic): The form of silica that is secreted by diatoms, radiolarians, silico-flagellates, and some sponges utilizing silica to create what amount to skeletal components.

Hydrometer: A device that measures the salinity of water. Two common designs are the floating hydrometer and the swing-arm hydrometer. In general, hydrometers do not provide the accuracy of results that salinometers and refractometers will, however they are often accurate enough for the purposes of most marine aquarium hobbyists.

Hyper Filtration: See Reverse Osmosis Filtration.

Ion Pair: The name given to a cation and anion joined by an ionic bond.

Ionic Bond: A bond in which one or more electrons transfer from one atom to another, and the resultant ions combine as a result of the attractions of opposite charges; ionic bonds differ from covalent bonds in that electrons are not shared between the ion pair.

Inductively Coupled Plasma-Atomic Emission Spectrometer (ICP-AES): A machine that determines the presence and abundance of elements in a (liquid) sample by observing the wavelength of light (corresponding to the specific element(s) of interest) and intensity emitted; this is accomplished by mixing the sample with argon gas that has been heated to plasma, which excites the electrons in the elements present, and then using an optical device to record and process the atomic emission data. Inexpensive ICP-AES systems cost upwards of $50,000, with more functional systems costing nearly twice that amount.

Kalkwasser: Aquarium trade name for calcium hydroxide.

Macroalgae: Designation given to complex marine plants such as seaweeds (which includes the numerous species of Caulerpa).

Macroporous Resin: A designation given to ion exchange resins possessing pores in the range of 200 to 500 Å; typically utilized in the removal of dissolved organic matter from solution.

Major Element: Any element in seawater which is found to exist at a concentration greater than 1 ppm. Elements present in the required concentration but which are predominantly in the form of dissolved gases or exhibit nutrient-type behavior are typically excluded from the list of major elements.

Marine Nitrogen Cycle: The oxidation of ammonium and nitrite into nitrate, and the reduction of nitrate to nitrogen gas, carried out by microbes.

Microalgae: Primitive plants possessing a very simple cell structure relative to the larger plants and algae.

Microporous Resin: A designation given to ion exchange resins possessing pores in the range of 20 to 50 Å; typically utilized in the selective exchange of cations and anions from solution.

Minor Element: Any element in seawater which is found to exist at a concentration less than 1 ppm but greater than 1 ppb.

Monochloramine: One of the three inorganic forms that chloramines take; each monochloramine molecule possesses one chloride ion. Monochloramine is the strongest biocide of the three inorganic forms.

Monovalent Ion: An ion having an electrical charge of positive or negative one; examples are sodium (Na^+) and chloride (Cl^-)

Nilsen Reactor: A vessel in which calcium hydroxide dissolves into incoming fresh water, with the resultant calcium- and hydroxide-rich solution being dosed into the aquarium as the pH in the aquarium water dictates. The benefits of this system are the addition of calcium ions and assistance in maintaining the pH of the aquarium water.

Nitrate: A molecule composed of one nitrogen and three oxygen ions, with the empirical formula NO_3^-. In aquatic environments, nitrate is largely produced by the microbial oxidation of nitrite.

Nitrification: The process in which ammonium is oxidized to form nitrite, and nitrite oxidized to form nitrate, carried out by microbes.

Nitrifier: Reference to the microbes responsible for the process of nitrification.

Nitrite: A molecule composed of one nitrogen and two oxygen ions, with the empirical formula NO_2^-. In aquatic environments, nitrite is largely produced by the microbial oxidation of ammonium.

Non-Conservative Behavior: Indicates that the concentration of the element in question is impacted by biological, chemical, and geological processes rather than physical processes.

Nutrient: A substance required for biological processes of primary producers; nutrients may be organic or inorganic.

Oxidation-Reduction Potential (ORP): The tendency for substances to lose or gain electrons (becoming reduced or oxidized, respectively) and consequently change chemical form.

Ozonation: The treatment of water with ozone gas as a means of killing microbes.

Ozone: A molecule composed of three oxygen atoms, with the empirical formula O_3. Ozone is a powerful oxidizing agent and is used primarily in marine aquaria to facilitate the rapid destruction of organic material; to do this, it is often injected into a protein skimmer or reaction vessel at a controlled rate in order to maintain a user-defined ORP level.

Particulate Organic Matter (POM): The organic matter in seawater that is present in a particulate form as opposed to being dissolved; the criterion that defines material as being particulate is that it cannot pass through a sieve possessing 0.4µm pores.

Permeate: The purified water that has passed through a reverse osmosis membrane.

Permeate Collection Material: In reverse osmosis water purification, the layer of material sandwiched between membrane layers that traps the permeate and shuttles it into the center pipe of the membrane.

pH: pH is formally defined as the negative log of the hydrogen ion activity (-log $\{H^+\}$). A more simplified explanation is essentially that pH is a measurement of the concentration of free hydrogen ions (H^+) in solution relative to that of free hydroxide ions (OH^-), or even more simply stated, pH is a measurement of a substance's acidity.

Phosphate: A molecule composed of one phosphorus atom and four oxygen atoms, with the empirical formula $(PO_4)^{3-}$.

Photosynthesis: A biochemical process in which water, nutrients, and a source of inorganic carbon are transformed in the presence of light into organic material and oxygen gas.

Phytoplankton: The autotrophic part of the plankton, organisms with poor swimming capabilities that are at the mercy of ocean currents.

Polyamide Polymer (PA): A material used to form reverse osmosis membranes. Incompatible with chlorine or chloramines, which must be filtered out of incoming water. Typically, PA membranes offer the highest removal rates of reverse osmosis membrane materials; they are also more expensive than CA membranes.

Polyvalent Ion: An ion having an electrical charge greater than positive or negative one; examples are calcium (Ca^{2+}) and aluminum (Al^{3+}).

Refractometer: In aquarium context, an optical instrument that measures the specific gravity of a liquid sample by comparing the refractive index to that of pure water.

Remineralization: The break down of particulate organic matter into the base constituents by microbes, or the dissolution of minerals (such as aragonite) into the water by biological, chemical, or geological processes.

Reverse Osmosis: A method of water purification in which source water is forced into contact with a semi-permeable membrane, with impurities (solutes) nearly-wholly rejected by the membrane and carried away in a percentage of the water (concentrate), and only purified water (permeate) passing through the membrane.

Salinity: The total concentration of dissolved inorganic substances present in a sample of water. Expressed in parts per thousand, or ‰.

Salinometer: An instrument that measures salinity by reading the electrical conductivity of a sample.

Scavenger: An animal that feeds upon organic material obtained from deceased animals or plants. Given the opportunity, most motile invertebrates and many fishes commonly kept in marine aquaria will act as scavengers.

Silica: A molecule composed of one silicon and two oxygen atoms, with the empirical formula SiO_2. Also referred to as silicon dioxide, silica is often used as a catch-all term to describe silicon-bearing molecules.

Silicate: The name given to metal oxides of silica, such as sodium silicate, Na_2SiO_3; for this reason, silicates are classified as salts.

Specific Gravity: The measurement of the density of a substance relative to that of pure water. Expressed as g/cm^3.

Strong Acid Cation Exchange Resins: Microporous ion exchange resins activated with hydrogen ions in order to remove cations with a greater charge from solution.

Strong Base Anion Exchange Resins: Microporous ion exchange resins activated with hydroxide ions in order to remove anions with a greater charge from solution.

Supplement: A substance utilized to alter the concentration of one or more target ions or other chemical parameters in an aquarium.

Thin Film Composite (TFC or TFM): A type of PA membrane material.

Titrimetric: Chemical analysis that relies on the completion of a chemical reaction between the concentration of a target substance in a sample and another substance in order to express the value of the target substance.

Total Dissolved Solids (TDS): The sum of conductive dissolved substances in solution. Expressed as ppm.

Trace Element: Any element in seawater which is found to exist at a concentration less than 1 ppb.

Trichloramine: One of the three inorganic forms that chloramines take; each trichloramine molecule possesses three chloride ions. Trichloramine is the weakest biocide of the three inorganic forms.

Zoochlorellae: A group of unicellular green algae that are found to live within the tissues of host organisms; the relationship between the host organism and the algae is symbiotic in that the algae gain protection from predation and provide a source of nutrients to the host through the exudation of organic material from their cells.

Zooplankton: The heterotrophic part of the plankton, organisms with poor swimming capabilities that are at the mercy of ocean currents.

Zooxanthellae : A group of golden-brown algae that are found to live within the tissues of host organisms; the relationship between the host organism and the algae is symbiotic in that the algae gain protection from predation and provide a source of nutrients to the host through the exudation of organic material from their cells.

Bibliography

Ford, T. E. ed. 1993.
Aquatic Microbiology: An Ecological Approach.
Blackwell Scientific, Oxford, 518 pp.

Fritz. J. S. and George H. Schenk. 1987.
Quantitative Analytical Chemistry
Allyn and Bacon, Boston, 690 pp.

Harris, D. C. 2003.
Quantitative Chemical Analysis
Freeman, New York, 901 pp.

Libes, S. M. 1992.
An Introduction to Marine Biogeochemistry.
John Wiley and Sons, Inc., New York, 734 pp.

Nybakken, J. W. 1993.
Marine Biology: An Ecological Approach.
Harper Collins, New York, 462 pp.

The Oceanography Course Team. 1999.
Seawater: Its Composition, Properties, and Behavior.
Butterworth-Heinemann, Oxford, 168 pp.

Pankow, J. F. 1991.
Aquatic Chemistry Concepts. Lewis, Chelsea, Michigan, 683 pp.

Valiela, I. 1995. *Marine Ecological Processes.*
Springer, New York, 686 pp.

Index

Note: Boldface numbers indicate illustrations; italic *t* indicates a table.

Photo Credits

ActinicBlue 156

Giangrande Alessia 248

Shironina Lidiya Alexandrovna 53

Annetje 241

CR Brightwell 14-5, 17, 20, 22, 28, 30-3, 36, 38, 40-2, 46, 48, 50, 52, 54-5, 60, 63, 67, 73-4, 76-8, 80-2, 85, 87-9, 92, 94, 96, 98, 100-1, 104, 106, 110-3, 116, 118, 121, 124-5, 127-9, 130-2, 134-6, 138, 140, 145-8, 150, 154, 158-9, 160, 164, 168-9, 172, 174, 180, 185-6, 192, 194-6, 200-3, 208, 211, 213-5, 217, 222-5

Stephen Coburn 1

Coko 10-1, 218

Stuart Elflett 70

Chistoprudov Dmitriv Gennadievich 188-9

Rui Manuel Teles Gomes 58

Johanna Goodyear 198

Tomasz Gulla 102-3

David Herlong 178

Ed Isaacs 244

Javarman 226-7

David Kelly 4-5

Bill Kennedy 242

Kristian 8-9, 246

Giuseppe Nocera 190

Morozova Oksana 18-9,

Paul 166

Nick Poling 228

Styve Reineck 179

Dennis Sabo 234

Dwight Smith 176-7

Razvan Stroie 12

Alex Teo Khek Teck 56

Trout55 206

Serdar Yagci 6, Cover

Andrejs Zavadskis 49

All other photos courtesy of TFH photo archives